Mikhail Bulgakov

Titles in the series Critical Lives present the work of leading cultural figures of the modern period. Each book explores the life of the artist, writer, philosopher or architect in question and relates it to their major works.

In the same series

Antonin Artaud *David A. Shafer*
Roland Barthes *Andy Stafford*
Georges Bataille *Stuart Kendall*
Charles Baudelaire *Rosemary Lloyd*
Simone de Beauvoir *Ursula Tidd*
Samuel Beckett *Andrew Gibson*
Walter Benjamin *Esther Leslie*
John Berger *Andy Merrifield*
Joseph Beuys *Claudia Mesch*
Jorge Luis Borges *Jason Wilson*
Constantin Brancusi *Sanda Miller*
Bertolt Brecht *Philip Glahn*
Charles Bukowski *David Stephen Calonne*
Mikhail Bulgakov *J.A.E. Curtis*
William S. Burroughs *Phil Baker*
John Cage *Rob Haskins*
Albert Camus *Edward J. Hughes*
Fidel Castro *Nick Caistor*
Paul Cézanne *Jon Kear*
Coco Chanel *Linda Simon*
Noam Chomsky *Wolfgang B. Sperlich*
Jean Cocteau *James S. Williams*
Salvador Dalí *Mary Ann Caws*
Guy Debord *Andy Merrifield*
Claude Debussy *David J. Code*
Gilles Deleuze *Frida Beckmann*
Fyodor Dostoevsky *Robert Bird*
Marcel Duchamp *Caroline Cros*
Sergei Eisenstein *Mike O'Mahony*
Michel Foucault *David Macey*
Mahatma Gandhi *Douglas Allen*
Jean Genet *Stephen Barber*
Allen Ginsberg *Steve Finbow*
Ernest Hemingway *Verna Kale*
Derek Jarman *Michael Charlesworth*
Alfred Jarry *Jill Fell*
James Joyce *Andrew Gibson*

Carl Jung *Paul Bishop*
Franz Kafka *Sander L. Gilman*
Frida Kahlo *Gannit Ankori*
Yves Klein *Nuit Banai*
Arthur Koestler *Edward Saunders*
Akira Kurosawa *Peter Wild*
Lenin *Lars T. Lih*
Stéphane Mallarmé *Roger Pearson*
Gabriel García Márquez *Stephen M. Hart*
Karl Marx *Paul Thomas*
Henry Miller *David Stephen Calonne*
Yukio Mishima *Damian Flanagan*
Eadweard Muybridge *Marta Braun*
Vladimir Nabokov *Barbara Wyllie*
Pablo Neruda *Dominic Moran*
Georgia O'Keeffe *Nancy J. Scott*
Octavio Paz *Nick Caistor*
Pablo Picasso *Mary Ann Caws*
Edgar Allan Poe *Kevin J. Hayes*
Ezra Pound *Alec Marsh*
Marcel Proust *Adam Watt*
John Ruskin *Andrew Ballantyne*
Jean-Paul Sartre *Andrew Leak*
Erik Satie *Mary E. Davis*
Arthur Schopenhauer *Peter B. Lewis*
Adam Smith *Jonathan Conlin*
Susan Sontag *Jerome Boyd Maunsell*
Gertrude Stein *Lucy Daniel*
Igor Stravinsky *Jonathan Cross*
Pyotr Tchaikovsky *Philip Ross Bullock*
Leon Trotsky *Paul Le Blanc*
Richard Wagner *Raymond Furness*
Simone Weil *Palle Yourgrau*
Tennessee Williams *Paul Ibell*
Ludwig Wittgenstein *Edward Kanterian*
Virginia Woolf *Ira Nadel*
Frank Lloyd Wright *Robert McCarter*

Mikhail Bulgakov

J.A.E. Curtis

REAKTION BOOKS

This book is dedicated, with deep love and pride,
to Miranda, Christopher and Adam

Published by Reaktion Books Ltd
Unit 32, Waterside
44–48 Wharf Road
London N1 7UX, UK
www.reaktionbooks.co.uk

First published 2017

Printed and bound in Great Britain by Bell & Bain, Glasgow

A catalogue record for this book is available from the British Library

ISBN 978 1 78023 741 1

Contents

Mikhail Bulgakov posing on the balcony of his apartment in Nashchokinsky Street in Moscow, 1935.

Prologue

... and the dead were judged from the things which were written in the books, according to their deeds.

Revelation 20:12, *New American Standard Version*

Mikhail Bulgakov's short life (1891–1940) spanned some of the most traumatic upheavals of modern history. Nostalgia for a world that had been irrevocably lost in the turmoil of the Russian Revolution was something that would accompany him throughout his career as a writer. It is a characteristic of his art that different periods of historical time are superimposed and explored within one and the same text. His artistic vision integrates different times and cultures in order to affirm his deeply held conviction that certain values are universal and eternal, although those values are rarely articulated with reference to received ideas about politics, philosophy or religion.

As in the epigraph from the Book of Revelation which he selected for his novel *The White Guard*, in Bulgakov's artistic world morality is defined by actions. Whether he is writing novels, short stories or plays, his creative vision is profoundly theatrical, in the sense that his reliance on dialogue underpins an art in which the acting out of dramatic action constitutes the plots of his works. The distressing experiences, both personal and political, endured by Russian intellectuals of his generation in the early decades of the twentieth century were often taboo subjects under the Bolshevik regime. Again and again, Bulgakov uses the device of 'dreaming' to open up visions of the world in which these traumas can be enacted for his contemporaries, or at least for posterity. The 'staging' of events in his art is inextricably interwoven with his own experiences of loss, persecution and censorship, and it is in this very broadest sense that Bulgakov's career can be summed up as having been 'a theatrical life'.

Medicine and Literature, 1891–1921

Kiev, 1891–1916

During his youth in Kiev as a schoolboy and as a medical student, Mikhail Bulgakov went to listen to Charles Gounod's opera *Faust* on as many as 41 separate occasions – he used to keep his opera tickets pinned up on the wall, and one of his sisters totted them all up. He would surely therefore have seen the great bass Fyodor Chaliapin, who visited Kiev to perform the role of Mephistopheles many times. This particular opera, based on Goethe's tragic verse drama about the scholarly Faust's pact with the Devil, came to acquire a kind of talismanic significance for him.

The whole Bulgakov family was passionate about opera, singing and classical music. Mikhail, the oldest of seven children, had an attractive baritone voice, and at one time yearned to become an opera singer: he was proud of a signed photograph he had from the bass star of the Kiev Opera, Lev Sibiriakov, which bore the inspirational inscription, 'Dreams sometimes turn into reality'. All the children sang, as well as playing the piano and other instruments; their father played the violin; and their mother would play Chopin for them at bedtime. Mikhail, who picked up the piano very easily after just a few lessons, loved to perform overtures or scenes from all his favourite operas: *Faust, Carmen, Ruslan and Liudmila,*

Fyodor Chaliapin as Mephistopheles in Charles Gounod's opera *Faust*, 1896.

The Barber of Seville, *La Traviata*, *Aida* and *Tannhäuser* – all the great works of nineteenth-century grand opera, many of which he came to know almost by heart.

Theatre was another great enthusiasm in the family: they attended the city's Russian-language theatres very regularly, and at home Mikhail led the way in performing charades and amateur dramatics. The family lived in a succession of rented apartments in Kiev, but in 1902 they also acquired a modest country *dacha* a day's journey away from Kiev, at Bucha. Their holidays there were spent running around barefoot, playing croquet, tennis and football, chess, draughts and whist, boating on the river, collecting beetles and butterflies and helping with the garden. But there was also writing and performing, and Mikhail started young: his first piece, *The Adventures of Svetlana*, was written at the age of seven, and he was always ready to improvise humorous verse about the dramas of family life for his brothers and sisters and their numerous friends. His mother and father each came from families of nine or ten children, and their own rowdy brood would later recall the years of their youth as having been dominated by laughter.

And then there were the books: all the Russian classics, naturally, including Pushkin, Chekhov (whose shorter comedies they used to stage at home), Tolstoy, Dostoevsky and Gor'ky. Mikhail was particularly fond of the Russian satirists such as Gogol' and Saltykov-Shchedrin. They were also familiar with many popular Western writers such as Charles Dickens, Victor Hugo, Mark Twain and Jerome K. Jerome, together with the fiction and plays of Guy de Maupassant, Maeterlinck, Ibsen, Knut Hamsun and Oscar Wilde. In other words, the family siblings formed a group of talented, highly cultured and well-educated young people. Towards the end of 1912, when Mikhail was twenty, he showed his sister Nadya his own first substantial stories, and declared to her with some confidence that he would become a writer.[1] However, this was a dream he would not fulfil for another decade or so, until he was thirty.

The Bulgakov family was not wealthy, but they had enough to live on quite comfortably, especially when the older children started supplementing the household's income by giving lessons. Mikhail's parents, Afanasy Bulgakov (1859–1907) and Varvara (née Pokrovskaya, 1869–1922), had married in July 1890 and their first child Mikhail (Misha) was born on 14 May 1891, succeeded by six siblings over the following eleven years: Vera, Nadezhda (Nadya), Varvara (Varya), Nikolay (Kolya), Ivan (Vanya) and Elena (Lyolya). Both of Mikhail's parents came from families of priests, and religion remained central to their lives. Varvara Bulgakova was very devout, and her husband was too: but it was striking that after he completed his studies at the Kiev Theological Academy in 1885, Afanasy Bulgakov had taken the decision not to enter the priesthood as such. Instead, he pursued the study of religion as

The Bulgakov children in the garden at Bucha in 1906 (clockwise from top: Mikhail, Varya, Nadya, Vanya, Lyolya, Kolya and Vera).

Afanasy Bulgakov (1859–1907), Mikhail's father.

an academic discipline, submitting a dissertation on the history of Methodism for a master's degree in 1887. That same year he was taken on at the Kiev Theological Academy as a Lecturer, where he soon established himself in the Department for the study of Western Christianity. His research publications continued to explore aspects of Methodism, as well as, for example, Freemasonry or recent developments in Catholic thought. It seems not unlikely that his father's intimate knowledge of Russian Orthodoxy, combined with his unusual openness to alternative ways of approaching the Christian faith, did much to shape the

Varvara Bulgakova with memorial portraits of her husband and of the family in mourning, in the sitting room at 13 Andreevsky Hill, 1908.

young Mikhail's outlook on religion. For Bulgakov as a writer, religion would come to figure not so much as a matter of dogma, but rather as a central dimension of a common European heritage, the defining feature of European civilization.

The young Mikhail's exceptionally happy childhood may be said to have come to an end at the age of fifteen, with the death of his father. Afanasy Bulgakov became seriously ill with malignant nephrosclerosis during the spring of 1906, when he was only in his late forties, and he had virtually lost his sight by September. His colleagues were so concerned about the future prospects of his family, the youngest of whom, Lyolya, was just four years old, that

Varvara Bulgakova and the children in mourning after the death of Afanasy Bulgakov, 1907.

Mikhail as a schoolboy in 1908.

they hastily arranged for his promotion to the rank of professor, which would secure him a larger pension. Within a month of his promotion Afanasy submitted his resignation on the grounds of ill health, and four days later, on 14 March 1907, he passed away. The loss of an admired father can naturally be traumatic for any adolescent at the age of fifteen, and sometimes bears particularly heavily on the oldest child. In Mikhail's case, it coincided with a period in his life when his own values and beliefs were undergoing huge changes, and his sister Nadya commented on the extent to which his uncompromising personality and sharp intelligence led to conflicts in the household:

> We argued a great deal in the family . . . about Darwin . . .
> We argued about politics, about the question of female
> emancipation and about women's education, about the
> English suffragettes, about the Ukrainian question, and
> about the Balkans: about science and religion, about
> philosophy, about non-resistance to evil and about the
> superman – we'd been reading Nietzsche.[2]

There were especially many disagreements with his mother, no doubt exacerbated by Mikhail turning away from the religious faith of his upbringing. In the spring of 1910, for example, he refused to fast for Lent. Nadya commented that he had 'evidently resolved the question of religion for himself – with non-belief. He's fascinated by Darwin.'[3]

Another source of tension for Mikhail emerged in the form of Ivan Voskresensky, the doctor who came to the house to treat Afanasy Bulgakov during 1906, and whose relationship with the professor's wife, seven years his senior, developed into a warm friendship and then a love affair. They did not in fact marry and live under the same roof until 1918, but he became a constant presence in the family. Mikhail was outraged, at least to begin

Varvara Bulgakova and Ivan Voskresensky, Mikhail's stepfather.

with. But his younger brother Nikolay, who became a medical researcher, would write to Ivan Voskresensky in 1922 to assure him that:

> The best and brightest memories are associated for me with your image, as someone who brought consolation to our family . . . It is difficult for me to express in words my deep gratitude for all that you did for mama in our difficult life, for our family, and for me at the beginning of my academic career.[4]

And Mikhail would also eventually find common ground with his unofficial stepfather, both in his lack of religious belief and also in his decision – perhaps an unexpected one in the light of his earlier aspiration to become a writer – to pursue medicine as a career.

In applying to study medicine at Kiev University in 1909, Bulgakov was following in the footsteps of two of his uncles on his mother's side, as well as those of his stepfather. But he proved to be a far from model student: it took him three attempts to pass his second-year exams, and he managed to complete his studies only in 1916. The main reason for his distractedness was a very attractive girl called Tasya (Tat'yana Nikolaevna Lappa, 1892?–1982), whom he first met in the summer of 1908 when she came to Kiev from the town of Saratov to visit her aunt. The seventeen-year-old Mikhail was asked to show her around the city, and they fell for each other to such an extent that his mother and her parents took alarm. After she returned home that autumn they intervened on more than one occasion to prevent the teenagers travelling to see each other. But three years later, in 1911, when Tasya had finished school, she moved to Kiev, ostensibly to become a student (she abandoned her studies after six months), although in reality it was to be with him. The two became inseparable, and spent as much time as they could having fun together, skating, going to the opera and the cinema, and drinking in cafés. In March 1913 Varvara Bulgakova wrote that Mikhail had completely ground her down over the previous winter, and the upshot was that he and Tasya were to marry on 26 April. Nadya commented that they were remarkably similar in the sheer irresponsibility of their characters, and indeed it appears that Tasya had become pregnant at this time and had to have an abortion.[5] Mikhail managed to scrape through that year's exams in time for the wedding, and a quiet ceremony was arranged, despite the very considerable reservations of the older generation. Mikhail marked the occasion by composing a comic playlet, in which he described how the two of them would have to live in the bathroom: he would sleep in the bath, and Tasya in the wash-basin.[6] Although the wedding went off well, Varvara Bulgakova took to her bed for a week afterwards. That autumn the young couple found somewhere to live on their own, but since they proved hopeless at managing a household budget and squandered money on restaurants and taxis, they still came to eat most of their meals with his mother at home.

Tat'yana Lappa (Tasya), 1910s.

The outbreak of the First World War occurred at a time when the couple had gone to Saratov to spend the summer with Tasya's parents. As a trainee doctor, Mikhail was immediately asked to help care for the wounded in the local hospital, and when they returned to Kiev in September 1914 so that he could continue his studies, Tasya volunteered there as a hospital nurse. Although he had not worked particularly hard during his first years at university, Mikhail completed his course in the spring of 1916 and qualified as a doctor 'with distinction'. On 4 April he applied to the Red Cross to be taken on as a volunteer. During the summer of 1916 he helped out in medical centres on the front line in

Mikhail Bulgakov, in 1916 or 1917.

southwestern Ukraine treating the Russian troops. Tasya was determined not to leave his side:

> Many of the injured there contracted gangrene, and he spent
> all his time sawing legs off. And I was there holding those legs
> . . . It made me feel so ill, I thought I was about to collapse . . .
> But then I got used to it.[7]

After this challenging experience, he was officially assigned that September to the post of district doctor in the small Russian village of Nikol'skoye in the Smolensk region, to the west of Moscow – all the more experienced doctors having been sent to take up front-line duties – and Tasya accompanied him there as well. It is this experience, of being thrust into a peasant community in the middle of nowhere, where as a barely qualified doctor he was expected to assume sole responsibility for the patients in his care, which is reflected in his cycle of stories called *Notes of a Young Doctor*.

Nikol'skoye and Vyaz'ma, 1916–18

Bulgakov apparently worked on these stories even while he was still in post at Nikol'skoye, and also when he was transferred after a year or so to the small nearby town of Vyaz'ma; and then he continued drafting them after his return to Kiev in February 1918. However, he only completed and published them as separate items in 1925–7, after he had already begun to establish himself as a writer. The cycle consists of seven semi-humorous short stories describing the newly qualified doctor's struggle to cope with the enormous professional challenges that are thrust upon him, together with one further story, 'Morphine'. In the form in which they are typically published today, the stories trace in chronological sequence the very junior doctor's arrival at the cottage hospital and his attempts to convince the trio of medical staff – and himself – of his competence. The early stories, 'The Embroidered Towel', 'The Steel Windpipe' and 'Baptism by Rotation', share a similar format, in which the doctor, secretly terrified, succeeds, through his medical training and great good luck, in dealing with the alarming medical emergencies with which he is confronted. In two other stories, 'The Snowstorm' and 'The Disappearing Eye', he ruefully recounts his own foolishness, firstly in setting out during a terrible blizzard and narrowly escaping some wolves, and subsequently in failing to understand that a little boy has not lost his eye, but is simply suffering from a huge boil, which has covered it over. In two other stories, however, 'Black as Egypt's Night' and 'The Starry Rash', his rapidly acquired but now extensive experience of the local population's health problems forces him to confront the underlying social issues that render them so intractable. These include the ignorance that almost causes the death of a miller, who swallows the entire prescription he has been given for malaria in one go, and the daunting lack of understanding of venereal diseases, which makes it so difficult to persuade patients in this remote province to see their treatment through.

The autobiographical underpinnings of these narratives are self-evident. Bulgakov himself spent a year in Nikol'skoye, was transferred to the town of Vyaz'ma at the end of 1917, and was demobilized in February 1918 on the grounds of ill health, after which he returned to his mother's in Kiev. The medical challenges, as well as many of the events and the emotions experienced by his fictional protagonist, are quite clearly based on Bulgakov's own adventures. Tasya recalled that they had barely managed to unpack on their first evening at Nikol'skoye when a woman in labour was brought in, providing Bulgakov with his very first experience of attending a childbirth, while Tasya stood beside him, looking up the relevant pages in the textbooks.[8] And a particular preoccupation with the uncontrolled spread of syphilis among the rural population, as reflected in the narrator's description of his attempts to set up a clinic in Nikol'skoye to address the problem, was something that Bulgakov himself shared. After his return to Kiev, he set up a private surgery in the family home as a doctor specializing in venereal and skin diseases.

The final story associated with the cycle *Notes of a Young Doctor* is 'Morphine'. Here too there is an autobiographical basis for the narrative, which describes in the form of a diary a young doctor's struggle with morphine addiction, which he first takes as a medical treatment for himself but then succumbs to as the overwhelming need of his waking hours. The fictional doctor resorts to shouting, threats, deceit and finally theft as he becomes helplessly dependent on the substance, and eventually he is driven to such despair and self-hatred that he shoots himself. Bulgakov endured much of this experience too. His wife Tasya described how in the spring of 1917 he first took morphine after he had accidentally infected himself while treating a child with diphtheria, and was then unable to stop. She was the one who had to carry his prescriptions to different chemists in his desperate attempts to get hold of more morphine, and it was she who endured his misery and his rages. He apparently kept notes about his state of mind throughout his struggle with the addiction. These later formed the basis for this story, which is harrowing in its utterly convincing diary account of the doctor's physical and mental torments. Eventually Tasya turned to Bulgakov's stepfather Ivan Voskresensky for advice when they returned to Kiev, and he helped her to substitute ampoules of distilled water for the morphine and so gradually wean him off his dependency.

However, while the essential content of all these stories is clearly rooted in personal experience, Bulgakov the author also took pains in 1925–7 to obscure the direct relationship between his protagonist's travails and his own. In the seven main stories that make up the cycle, the narration is delivered in the first person, in a voice clearly corresponding closely to Bulgakov's own, and reflects authentically his apprehensiveness upon assuming his new responsibilities, his longing to be in a more civilized environment, and his exasperation at the foolish ignorance and obstinacy of his rural patients. But at the same time, Bulgakov takes pains to confuse the reader as to the exact correlation of the biographical facts of his protagonist's life with his own. For one thing, the entire chronology is shifted forward a year. Bulgakov arrived at Nikol'skoye in September 1916, his protagonist only in September 1917. Furthermore, it is not the civilized world of Bulgakov's home town of Kiev, but the Russian capital, Moscow, that the fictional doctor longs for, together with nights spent at the Bol'shoi Theatre there, listening to *Aida*. The most notable difference, however, is the absence of Tasya from the narrative: she who had done so much to care for him, support him in his work and save him from the demon of addiction, is entirely written out of the fictional story. Instead, the young doctor here talks constantly of his utter loneliness. As for the story 'Morphine', the focus of biographical identification is even further distanced. Bulgakov's fictional doctor acquires a name – Dr Bomgard – and late in 1917 he has been transferred, to his great delight, back to the gleaming, modern hospitals of Moscow (this is one of the several ways in which this story fails to fit into the chronological structure of the other seven stories). There he receives a message in February 1918 from his successor at Nikol'skoye, a former fellow-student called Dr Polyakov. It is Polyakov who has succumbed to morphine addiction, tracing the course of his nightmare in a notebook which he bequeaths to Bomgard after his suicide, and which Bomgard then publishes. Thus the Bomgard/Bulgakov figure simply provides the frame narrative for the confession of an addiction suffered by an entirely different character.[9]

There is virtually no evidence in the form of surviving drafts of any of these stories to allow us to establish at what stage these devices to mask the identification of protagonist with author were conceived: whether they were always intended to be there, or whether they were introduced at the time of publication because of the political changes which had transformed Russia in the intervening years, from the First World War until after the death of Lenin. Did Bulgakov, who by 1925–7 was established in Soviet Moscow as a writer, feel it would be wiser not to draw attention too blatantly to his own role and actions as a young doctor trained in Tsarist Kiev during the years of war, revolutions and civil war? And since he had by then remarried, perhaps it also seemed more tactful not to dwell on the importance of his first wife Tasya to him during those years (true, the stories are perhaps also all the more gripping for presenting the protagonist as being entirely alone). One theme that is almost entirely absent from these stories, even though they cover the years from 1916 to 1918, is indeed that of the February and October Revolutions of 1917. These are scarcely alluded to in the seven main stories, where the protagonist's situation is above all defined by his being cut off from the events of the outside world. It is only in 'Morphine' that there are explicit allusions to it. On 2 March 1917, Dr Polyakov notes: 'Rumours about something grandiose. Apparently Nicholas II has been overthrown' (I, 142).[10] By mid-November he has made a half-hearted attempt to seek treatment for his addiction in Moscow, and uses the recent disturbances and shooting during the October Revolution as a feeble excuse for his lack of resolve. He abandons the attempt and returns to Nikol'skoye: 'Moscow, which is in upheaval, rebellious Moscow is far, far away. And I am not in the least concerned about any of it' (I, 150, 153).

Bulgakov and Tasya did indeed feel very cut off from the events of 1917. Within five days of the Bolshevik coup against the moderately socialist Provisional Government on 25 October,

Tasya wrote to Nadya, who had been taking exams in Moscow, asking her for news: 'Please write immediately to tell us what is happening in Moscow. We live here in complete ignorance, and for four days now we've had no news from anywhere. We're very anxious, and we're in a terrible state.'[11] In early December 1917 Bulgakov went to Moscow himself, in order to try and gain release from his post on medical grounds (because of what he claimed was nervous exhaustion) but without success; on the same trip he travelled to Saratov to visit Tasya's parents. On New Year's Eve he wrote a very revealing letter from Vyaz'ma to Nadya, who was now living with her husband in Tsarskoye Selo, near Petrograd (formerly St Petersburg):

My only consolation is my work, and my reading in the evenings. I fondly read old-fashioned authors (whatever I can find, as there are not many books here), and I rejoice in their depictions of the good old days. Ah, why was I born so late! Why was I not born a hundred years ago? But of course it's impossible to remedy that! I long desperately to get out of here, to Moscow or to Kiev, where at least life is still going on, even if it is fading. I would particularly like to be in Kiev! The New Year will begin in two hours' time. What will it bring me? I was sleeping just now, and I dreamed of Kiev, of familiar and beloved faces, I dreamed that someone was playing the piano . . . Will the old times return? The present is such that I try to live without paying any attention to it . . . without seeing or hearing it! Not long ago on a trip to Moscow and to Saratov I was forced to see it all with my own eyes, and I would prefer not to see any more of it. I saw the grey mobs breaking the windows of the trains with whooping and foul cursing, I saw them beating people. In Moscow I saw buildings which had been wrecked and burnt . . . Dumb, bestial faces . . . I saw mobs besieging the entrances of the banks which had been seized and closed down, queues of hungry people at the shops, pitiful, persecuted officers, and I saw newssheets in which essentially they are only writing about one thing: about the blood which is flowing in the south and in the west and the east, and about prisons. I saw everything with my own eyes, and I understood once and for all what had taken place (VIII, 16–17).

This had clearly been a chastening experience. Bulgakov's letter to Nadya conveys several preoccupations that he would carry forward into his life as a writer: his revulsion at the mindless violence of the unenlightened mob, and his doubts about the political values of the Bolshevik Revolution. There is also a yearning, not just for the affectionate, cultured world of his previous family life, but also for an earlier age, as represented in the innocent pleasure of nineteenth-century tales of adventure (in the stories, his narrator refers to having read Fenimore Cooper, *Robinson Crusoe* and Sherlock Holmes). As so often in Bulgakov's writing, the realm of sleep and dreams frees him to travel to other places and other times: indeed, he concludes his story 'Black as Egypt's Night' with the words: 'Dreams are a great thing! . . .' (I, 110).

Kiev, 1918–19

Kiev cherishes its historic role as the cradle of the Russian Orthodox faith in the region, ever since the tenth-century Prince Vladimir of Kiev converted to Christianity and required his subjects to follow suit. All this took place long before any kind of Russian state – or even the city of Moscow – had come into existence. Ukraine's later status as part of the Tsarist Russian Empire dates largely from the eighteenth century. But Kiev then became one of the major cities within that empire, and many of its wealthier citizens were Russians for whom the Ukrainian language came second. The Bulgakov family was typical of the well-established

Russian middle class there. As Nadya put it: 'Although we lived in Ukraine (and later we all learned to speak Ukrainian), we nevertheless all had a purely Russian education. And we very much felt ourselves to be Russian. But we loved Ukraine.'[12]

At the outbreak of the First World War in 1914, the population of Ukraine, whether ethnically Russian or Ukrainian, was mobilized as part of the regular Russian army. Then came the abdication of Tsar Nicholas II as a consequence of the February Revolution in 1917. But after the Bolsheviks had overthrown the Provisional Government in the October Revolution that same year, Lenin and Trotsky created a Red Army which battled on several fronts, including in Ukraine, against the remnants of the Russian Tsarist forces, the 'White' Army led by pro-monarchist generals. At the same time, however, in order to consolidate their power and in the name of international worker solidarity, the Bolsheviks resolved in March 1918 (very shortly after Bulgakov's return to Kiev) to pull Russia out of the First World War. The Treaty of Brest-Litovsk, signed on 3 March, effectively represented a capitulation to the Germans and their allies. According to its punitive terms, Russia ceded to the Germans its control over Poland, Finland, Estonia, Latvia, Lithuania and Belarus as well as Ukraine, thereby losing close to one-quarter of the population and a significant proportion of the richest industrial resources and agricultural land of the former Russian Empire. Thanks to the actions of their own new government, the people of Kiev thus suddenly found themselves in the spring of 1918 subject to the Germans, whom they had been fighting for the previous four years. More specifically, the Germans set up a puppet government, called the Hetmanate, to control this vast, newly acquired territory. By November, the German collapse and the signing of the Armistice led to the Germans withdrawing from Ukraine, and the Hetman Skoropadsky fled with them. In December 1918 the Ukrainian nationalist forces of Symon Petlyura seized power in Kiev, although the Bolsheviks were also advancing rapidly on the city. This chaotic situation, with the Germans and the Hetmanate fleeing the Red Army, which in turn was battling against the monarchist Whites as well as Petlyura's Ukrainian nationalists, lasted from 1917 until 1921. Bulgakov recalled this confused tussle for power in the Civil War period as follows:

> The inhabitants of Kiev reckon that there were eighteen changes of power. Some stay-at-home memoirists counted up to twelve of them. I can tell you that there were precisely fourteen, and what's more I personally lived through ten of them.[13]

This turbulent period in Bulgakov's life really begins in February 1918, when he was at last successful in his request to be released from his post as a country doctor, and returned to the family home in Kiev. He and Tasya had been almost entirely cut off from the military and political convulsions that had utterly transformed life in Ukraine during the eighteen months he had been away. The political status and identity of his home city of Kiev had altered in his absence, and was about to change even more dramatically again with the annexation of Ukraine by the Germans. But his family had had to live through all the events of those dangerous and unpredictable months in the city. Shortly before the revolutionary violence that Bulgakov had glimpsed in Moscow, his mother and his brother Kolya (who at nineteen had only just joined the Russian army as a cadet) had themselves had a frightening experience in Kiev. Varvara Bulgakova described to Nadya their adventures as the regular army came under attack from workers and Bolshevik soldiers in the days immediately following the October 1917 coup:

> On the night of the 29th . . . we were literally a hair's breadth away from death . . . When the crossfire began, with shooting

The Bulgakov home at 13 Andreevsky Hill in Kiev.

at the School and from it, we found ourselves in the firing-zone and the bullets were smacking against the very wall where we were standing. Fortunately there was an officer among some casual passers-by (about six people) who were endeavouring to take cover from the bullets; he ordered us to lie down on the ground, as close to the wall as we could. We endured a dreadful hour: the machine-guns were chattering away as well as the rifle shots, the bullets clattering against the wall, and then they were joined by the thudding of the shells . . . But evidently our time had not yet come, and Kolya and I survived (one woman was killed); but we will never forget that night . . . Poor boy, he was so alarmed on my behalf, and I on his . . .

Later that night Kolya rejoined his unit, and his mother was escorted home through the darkness to return to the rest of her family, having made the sign of the cross over Kolya and kissed him hard as they parted.[14]

Bulgakov's mother was still living with the younger children in the family home at 13 Andreevsky Hill, which they had occupied since 1906 or 1907.[15] This house, now well known as the site of the Bulgakov Museum in Kiev, occupies a very striking position on an exceptionally wide, long and steep cobbled street that curves sharply from the top of the hill down to the district of Podol. So steep is the incline that the house has three floors as you approach it from below; and yet the entrance to the Bulgakovs' apartment on the top floor is through a courtyard at the back reached directly from the same level as the street higher up the hill. This was the home immortalized as no. 13 Alekseevsky Hill in Bulgakov's novel *The White Guard*, where its cream-coloured blinds, its library of favourite books, the piano and the old-fashioned tiled stove create a secure environment for the family while the turmoil of civil war seethes outside. Bulgakov and Tasya settled back here, and he used one of the rooms in the apartment to set up his private doctor's practice. As a non-combatant, Bulgakov might have hoped to ride out the various changes of power in the city unscathed, although in fact it turned out that he was vulnerable to being mobilized for medical service by the successive forces that occupied the city.

The White Guard, which like *The Notes of a Young Doctor* was written some years after the events it describes, is another patently autobiographical work in the Bulgakov canon. Quite apart from the lovingly described home which is the setting for much of the action, the family whose story is told in the novel represents a condensed version of Bulgakov's own. But one very major change reflects his family's history in the period between the events of 1918–19, which form the subject of the text, and the moment when Bulgakov was describing them in the early 1920s. This was the death of Varvara Bulgakova, which in reality occurred in 1922, but here is transposed to May 1918, to form the starting point of the narrative. The fictional mother's body has been laid to rest in the cemetery alongside their professor father, who has died long before. Their three grieving adult children, who remain behind in the apartment, are a young doctor, Aleksei Turbin (28), Yelena (24) and Nikol'ka (seventeen). Aleksei, the eldest, has recently 'returned after onerous campaigns, service and misfortunes, to Ukraine, to the City, and to his own home' (II, 83). The 'City' is never named in the novel, but is unmistakably Kiev with its recognizable streets and churches, and the statue of St Vladimir brandishing a cross on the top of the hill in the park. Aleksei, despite being in many respects the central protagonist of the novel, remains to some extent a shadowy figure. This will often be the case in those works of Bulgakov's where a semi-autobiographical figure takes centre stage. We will hear nothing more of Aleksei's mysterious misfortunes (perhaps a private allusion to Bulgakov's addiction), nor will we ever see him acting very decisively. For much of the novel Aleksei will be caught unawares by events as they happen, and later on will be lying wounded and delirious in bed for the entire duration of Petlyura's occupation of Kiev. Instead, the noble, heroic figure is the younger brother Nikol'ka, who has an acute sense of honour and a brave, impulsive character that leads him towards danger, adventure and love. Their sister, the 'golden' Yelena, is the guardian of the hearth: devout, generous and loving as well as very beautiful, she provides a focus for the honourable deeds and amorous attentions of the family's officer friends. She has, however, perhaps committed an error of judgement in marrying the creepy Tal'berg, an opportunist who has so far succeeded in positioning himself to advantage with each successive change of political power in the 'City'. Most recently, he has found himself a post as a member of the Hetman's entourage. However, as 1918 draws to a close and the end of the First World War leads to the Germans withdrawing from Ukraine, Tal'berg seizes the opportunity to escape the city with them and with the Hetman, leaving his wife and her brothers behind. As Tal'berg hastily departs, Nikol'ka is proud enough to remain silent. Aleksei also says nothing, but only 'because he is a rag of a man' (II, 106).

The Turbin brothers and their fellow officers now find themselves in a dangerous and confusing plight. Their natural loyalty is to the old regime and to the tsar, but in July 1918 the Bolsheviks had taken the decision to execute the tsar and his family, in order to diminish the appeal of the White movement; the White armies, which still represent the monarchist cause, are in chaos, or in cowardly retreat. During 1918 the several months of the German-dominated Hetmanate have in fact brought relative peace to the city, but their withdrawal leaves it exposed to the threat of violence from Petlyura's Ukrainian nationalist forces, while on their heels comes the Red Army, anxious to seize back for the Bolshevik state the territory ceded to the Germans at Brest-Litovsk. Neither of these two groups has any sympathy for the Russian bourgeoisie of Kiev. These young people and their friends face the threat of violence, and no longer have any external authority to turn to. Instead, they draw upon their inner reserves, epitomized in their family values of honour, love and loyalty, together with the safe haven of the well-lit apartment. Nikol'ka will continue to play his guitar; arias from *Faust* and other operas will still be played on the piano to conjure up the eternal power of art over the transitory events of political life; and they will face any trouble together:

> Never. Never pull the lampshade off the lamp. The lampshade is sacred. Never run away, scurrying like a rat away from danger towards the unknown. Sit and doze under the lampshade, read a book – and let the snow-storm howl. Wait for them to come to you (II, 102).

Such images of light and dark pervade the entire text, repeatedly suggesting the threat that the forces of darkness offer to the civilized world of the family. The constant references to the lighting of given episodes also contribute to what may be described as the unexpected 'theatricality' of this novel, perhaps the most interesting and innovative aspect of its poetics. Bulgakov indicated in his manuscript that this novel about Kiev in 1918–19 had been completed in 1923–4 in Moscow, not so very long after the events he describes. And yet the momentousness of the political and social transformations his country has undergone in that brief interim, not to mention the complete upheaval in his personal affairs, prompt him to look back at this world as something far distant, and irrevocably lost. When seeking a means of conveying this to the reader, he opted for a set of devices that would underline his sense that he could only conjure the events by presenting them as 'staged' action, as a performance. This leitmotif is first introduced parodically, when the unprincipled Tal'berg keeps using the word 'operetta' to indicate his scorn for each of the successive authorities that take over in Kiev, whether it is the Hetmanate of which he has formed a part, but which is collapsing with the withdrawal of the Germans, or the Bolshevik regime in Moscow, or Petlyura's forces (II, 102–5): indeed, the election of the Hetman had itself taken place in a circus ring, suggesting its 'staged' nature. Even the recruitment centre for the doomed Russian forces, where Aleksei signs up to help them defend the city against Petlyura, is situated on Theatre Street, behind the opera house, and he is recruited by a colonel sitting on 'a sort of stage' (II, 153, 157). The Turbin family, on the other hand, live by their devotion to true culture, to opera: the score of *Faust* is ever open on the piano, neglected only at the worst moments of Aleksei's illness, and in particular they favour Valentin's baritone aria, in which the brother setting off to war prays to God to protect his sister. This was an aria that Bulgakov himself loved to sing: and perhaps this baritone voice, conjuring ideals of family, devotion and honour, is a reflection of Bulgakov's most cherished convictions. Aleksei too reads events through the prism of operatic characters: the snowy city at night reminds him of

Rimsky-Korsakov's operatic setting of a Gogol' story. Similarly, the narrator compares one of the officers to Radamès (from *Aida*), while another's gauntlets remind him of Marcel's from Meyerbeer's *Les Huguenots*. When Shervinsky, formerly a supporter of the Hetman, decides hastily to adopt a new identity, it is as an elegant opera singer in bow tie and shiny shoes – which will make him all the more attractive to Yelena. And at the end of the novel, when Nikol'ka hastily wipes away all the defiant political declarations that had been scribbled on the tiled stove, the only words he leaves behind are a message to Yelena to say that there will be tickets for *Aida*.

Other aspects of *The White Guard* which lend it a certain theatricality form part of its very construction as a text. The novel is effectively made up of a succession of scenes, introduced by their settings (the apartment, the recruiting office, the School, the square by the cathedral and so on); and the protagonists are introduced according to their age, physical appearance and garb (on a number of occasions costume-changes take place to mark someone's self-disguise for political considerations, to escape danger). The narrative voice fluctuates and varies throughout, but the text is ultimately dominated by dialogue: an extreme example of this is the scene in the cathedral square, where a hubbub of different voices offers contradictory opinions about Petlyura. Characters are basically defined by their words, and through their actions. This chimes with the message offered by the work's second epigraph, the quotation from the Book of Revelation about the dead being judged according to their deeds – a message which is reinforced by God's comment in Aleksei's dream that what matters is not faith, since 'all of you commit the same deeds' (II, 149). What is really lacking from this novel is any kind of psychological analysis or authorial comment, such as we might have expected from a traditional historical novel of the nineteenth century, as for instance in Tolstoy's *War and Peace*, one of the well-thumbed books in the Turbin household.

The Bulgakov sitting room at 13 Andreevsky Hill, with the tiled stove in the corner, 1980s.

As a substitute for this psychological analysis, we are offered an insight into certain characters' minds through the device of dreams. Aleksei endures a nightmare in which a Dostoevskian demon mocks the idea that Russians could live according to a code of honour (II, 127); and later he has the dream in which he is offered a vision of heaven where even the atheist Bolsheviks can be accommodated, since all that matters is deeds, not faith.

This same dream is also a curiously prophetic one, since it shows him not just the forthcoming death of the honourable Nai-Turs, Nikol'ka's hero, but even the consequences of an event still far in the future, the battle between the Reds and the Whites for the Crimean isthmus of Perekop in 1920. What is striking about this dream is that Aleksei never makes any reference to it in his waking life – so that in fact we are left uncertain as to whether it is some kind of Freudian projection of his own genuine, deep-seated fears and beliefs, or whether it is just a narratorial device, a sleight-of-hand allowing the author to introduce effectively 'unattributed' opinions and themes to his fiction. Nikol'ka and Yelena also experience more than one dream, and indeed the entire novel concludes with a dreamscape of the city, encompassing the dreams of all the principal protagonists but culminating in the innocent, playful dreaming of a small child.

The prevalence of dreams in the novel in turn contributes to our sense of the artifice, the unreality of all that is going on. After the buffoonery of the Hetmanate, the next threat to the city comes from Petlyura – and yet throughout the entire novel and even during the 47 days in which his forces remain in power on this occasion, from December 1918 into 1919, he is never seen in person. Instead, it is suggested that he may even be 'simply a myth, engendered in Ukraine by the mists of the terrible year 1918' (II, 141). Despite its all-too-real brutality, directed especially at the Jewish population, Petlyura's army similarly appears to have 'been woven out of the frosty mist' (II, 246). By the time Aleksei has recovered from his delirium, Petlyura's forces are abandoning the city again, and he wonders whether Petlyura was ever really there: 'Or did I dream it all? I don't know, and it's impossible to verify' (II, 355). These comments serve to underline the apparent contingency of historical events, and the difficulty of distinguishing between physical reality and the visions of hallucination or dream.

In terms of the highly teleological ideology of the Soviet state, with its Marxist insistence upon the historical inevitability of the coming of the dictatorship of the proletariat, Bulgakov's views on history were clearly unacceptable. Instead of focusing upon human agency, and upon the obligations placed upon the individual to act in the interests of class conflict, Bulgakov in *The White Guard* presents us with a deeply sympathetic portrait of a doomed class, of their values and their way of life. The novel is framed by narratorial comments in its opening and closing pages which present a fatalistic view of life. At the beginning, Nikol'ka rails against the injustice of their mother's death: 'But Nikol'ka did not yet know that whatever happens is always as it should be, and is only for the best' (II, 84). This is a sentiment that Bulgakov's character Woland will reiterate a decade later in *The Master and Margarita*. Equally, the novel ends with a glimpse of the statue of St Vladimir, in which the cross he brandishes appears more like a sword: 'But it is not frightening. Everything will pass. Suffering, torments, blood, hunger and pestilence. The sword will melt away, but the stars will remain when no shadow of our bodies or our deeds remains on this earth' (II, 372). Not surprisingly, this quasi-mystical message of reconciliation with suffering, together with Bulgakov's emphasis on the transience of human actions, found little favour with the authorities. The publication of this novel in the journal *Russia* was halted before it had even been completed, and the text did not appear as a complete work in Soviet Russia until 1966, 26 years after Bulgakov's death. The projected further two parts to what he had originally conceived as a historical and autobiographical trilogy had to be abandoned. But aptly, when he did ultimately return to this same subject-matter, Bulgakov reworked it not through the medium of prose, but in the form of stage plays for the theatre.

After Bulgakov and Tasya returned to the flat at no. 13 Andreevsky Hill in February 1918, where his mother was living

Mikhail Bulgakov's sister Varvara (Varya).

with Vera and the three younger children and their cousin, Konstantin, they were soon joined by Varya and her husband, Leonid Karum. Bulgakov was using one room for his surgery. It began to feel very crowded, and by the end of the summer Varvara Bulgakova decided to go up the hill to no. 38, moving in with Ivan Voskresensky and taking her youngest, Lyolya, with her. The couple evidently married at this point, but some of her children did not discover this until they saw her new surname on her gravestone. The household down at no. 13 was therefore made up in the winter of 1918–19 exclusively of young people, just as in the novel. Money was quite tight, and Varya's husband Karum would grumble that Bulgakov didn't pull his weight, and that he and Tasya were too extravagant. In evoking their lives during those months in *The White Guard*, Bulgakov reflected the tension between the two men by parodying Karum in the figure of Tal'berg, much to the annoyance of his sister Varya. In truth, Karum was a devoted husband and father, and although he did leave the city with the Hetman, he returned almost immediately. Bulgakov's somewhat ruthless exploitation of real-life prototypes in his fiction also extended to the Turbins' comical downstairs neighbour Vasilisa, whose original, Vasily Listovnichy, was a respectable architect who perished in the summer of 1919 trying to escape from detention by the Reds.[16]

There is not much documentary evidence to reflect the Bulgakov family's lives during 1918, but the range and the consistency of the themes addressed in a number of Bulgakov's fictional works evoking this period are such as to persuade any reader of their basis in lived experience. While *The White Guard* focuses primarily on the end of 1918 and the imminent arrival of Petlyura that December as the Germans withdrew, a number of other works seem to have been prompted by the traumatic experience Bulgakov suffered in early February 1919, when Petlyura's men in turn abandoned Kiev to the Red Army. A particular episode, which also features briefly in *The White Guard*, recurs more than once in his short stories. In 'On the Night of the Second' (1922) it takes place in freezing weather on the second of February, at a bridge over the river not far from the Bulgakov home. Petlyura's Ukrainian nationalist troops threaten a doctor, and he hears the chilling, high-pitched screams of a Jew being tortured, watching helplessly as the man is beaten to death in the snow. He fantasizes a scenario in which he executes the brutal torturers. The doctor exclaims to himself: 'I may be a monarchist by conviction. But at this precise moment what are needed here are the Bolsheviks . . . Lord . . . Grant that the Bolsheviks should descend upon this bridge this minute' (ii, 29). The doctor is made to go with Petlyura's troops as they retreat, and only by a miracle manages to slip away from them and escape. By the time he returns to his home on the hill, where his brother and sister have been anxiously waiting with their singer friend, his hair has turned white. The doctor reproaches himself for his powerlessness: 'I'm a fool. I'm a pitiful bastard . . . I am a member of the despicable intelligentsia' (ii, 29, 41). Tasya recounted how Bulgakov himself had been forcibly mobilized by Petlyura's men, precisely when the Bolsheviks were imminently expected:

> Between two and three in the morning there was such a ringing at the door! Varya and I rushed to open it, and of course it was him. For some reason he had been running very hard, he was trembling all over, and he was in a terrible state – all nervy. We put him to bed, and after that he stayed in bed for a week, he was ill. Afterwards he told us how he had somehow managed to lag behind a little, then a little bit more, then slipped behind a column, and then further on to another, and then rushed away down an alley at a run. He ran so fast that his heart was pounding, and he thought he would have a heart attack. That scene, of a man being killed by the bridge, was something he saw himself, and he kept recalling it.[17]

In 'The Raid' (1923) the Jewish victim caught while on sentry duty survives to become a librarian in later life, and to tell his tale to a group of colleagues who had assumed that this frail man could never have fought in the war. In a further story, 'I Have Killed' (1926), yet another doctor protagonist recalls the events of February 1919 in Kiev: he is forcibly mobilized from his home on 'Alekseevsky' Hill by Petlyura's army as they retreat, and obliged to tend their men. But when they condemn a woman to a fearsome beating after she has protested about their killing of her husband, he shoots their commander in cold blood. Despite this flagrant breach of the Hippocratic oath, in this fiction at least the doctor has had the courage to act upon his moral indignation.

This experience inaugurates in Bulgakov's fiction a preoccupation with issues of guilt and cowardice. Time and time again his principal male protagonists fall short of outright heroism, and torment themselves with remorse. We may recall again that slightly unexpected description of Aleksei Turbin in *The White Guard* as 'a rag of a man'. But there is yet another source of the theme of guilt in Bulgakov's fiction which may have autobiographical underpinnings, and that is a sense of guilt towards the mother, focused specifically around a failure to look after a younger brother. Here the origins may lie in the events of the later part of 1919, rather than the beginning of the year. It seems that the seizure of the city of Kiev by the Red Army in February that year was succeeded by a period of relative calm, rather confirming the fictional doctor's opinion that they would at least be more welcome than Petlyura's men. During August 1919, there was a sudden threat that Petlyura's forces would recapture the city, and Bulgakov and some of his siblings simply hid away in a barn in the country for a couple of weeks until the danger had passed. But instead, the city very soon fell to the Whites once more. And here disillusionment with the forces who might have seemed closest to the Bulgakovs' own values set in even more strongly.

After the fiasco of their failure to defend the city at the end of 1918, the Whites now returned and instituted a series of searches and interrogations, further alienating their erstwhile supporters. Nevertheless, it seems that Bulgakov did agree voluntarily to be mobilized by them that autumn, and he was immediately despatched to the North Caucasus to serve as a medical officer for their forces in the town of Vladikavkaz (he also spent time in the towns of Grozny and Beslan).[18] We do not know the exact sequence of events, but Bulgakov's brothers Kolya and Vanya seem to have left Kiev with the White forces that autumn as well. For a long time their mother had little idea what had happened to them, but then it emerged that the two younger men had withdrawn towards the south as the Whites retreated, and travelled on as émigrés, settling initially in Zagreb, and then in Paris. Neither Kolya nor Vanya would see any of their family, nor their home city, ever again.

Bulgakov wrote another short story, 'The Red Crown' (1922), in which the protagonist lacerates himself for his failure to look after his brother Kolya. (Nikolai/Nikol'ka/Kolya is the younger brother's name in all these stories, and is of course the name of Bulgakov's own brother.) The mother has enjoined him as the eldest, and as one who loves the nineteen-year-old Kolya, to bring him back from the fighting. The narrator finds his brother, who promises to come with him after just one more mission, but he reappears with a terrible, fatal head wound (the 'red crown' of the title). Now confined to a mental asylum, the narrator is haunted every night by his brother, who appears before him reproachfully: only once does he have a happy dream of him still at home, playing a piano on which there stands a score of *Faust*. It seems likely that this story was written very shortly after the news had reached him of his mother's sudden death from typhus at the age of 52, which occurred at the beginning of February 1922. Only in January 1922 had the family in Kiev received a letter from Kolya in Zagreb to confirm that he was in fact alive.[19] But when Bulgakov had last visited his mother in Kiev in September 1921, there had still been no news of him or Vanya for about two years. Like his narrator, Bulgakov may have felt he was guilty of sins of omission as well as commission as far as his mother and his siblings were concerned.

One final cause for guilt – and a trigger for insanity – that is mentioned in 'The Red Crown' appears to be another episode that Bulgakov may have witnessed in real life, perhaps in the town of Berdyansk, en route from Kiev to the Caucasus. It is another episode of violence, but in this instance the instigator is not one of Petlyura's henchmen but a White commander, who hangs a workman from a lamppost on suspicion of being a Bolshevik sympathizer. 'I went away, so as not to see a man being hanged, but fear came away with me, in my shaking legs' says the narrator, who later fantasizes an alternative scenario in which he would have stepped forward and prevented the White commander from acting in such a ferocious way (II, 43). This is a theme that would be developed to its full extent in Bulgakov's play *Flight* (1926–8).

The Caucasus, 1919–21

Bulgakov travelled to Vladikavkaz in the late summer or early autumn of 1919 as a military doctor mobilized by the White Army, and two weeks after his arrival he sent a telegram summoning Tasya to join him there. He may well have felt that this mobilization by the Whites was the least bad option in the circumstances, and his pro-White political position with regard to the Bolsheviks at that particular moment was set out fairly unequivocally in an article he published in November 1919 for a newspaper in Grozny. It was clearly much influenced by the mood of those around him at the time. The piece, 'Prospects for the Future', is prompted by an English illustrated magazine he had recently perused, in which the photographs reflect the energy of post-war recovery in the West.

> Day in, day out, colossal machines in colossal factories are feverishly devouring coal, roaring and pounding, pouring out streams of molten metal, forging, repairing and building things . . . They are forging the might of peace, replacing those machines that only recently, sowing death and destruction, forged the might of war. In the West the Great War between great peoples is at an end. And they are now healing their wounds. And of course they will recover, they will recover in no time at all! (II, 20)

But meanwhile in Russia, the White armies face a massive task in trying to wrest the country back from Trotsky and his followers, and Bulgakov deplores those who sit back and criticize the Bolsheviks, but do nothing to contribute to the fight. He predicts that the battle will be hard-fought, and victory will be achieved only very slowly:

> And who will see those bright days? Will it be us? Oh, no! Our children perhaps, or perhaps our grandchildren, for the sweep of history is broad, and history 'reads' decades as easily as it does individual years. And we, the representatives of an unlucky generation, will die like pitiful bankrupts, forced to tell our children: 'You pay, pay the debt off honourably, and never forget the social revolution!' (II, 22)

This is Bulgakov at his most conservatively patriotic, and his prophecies for his country are bitter ones – and largely accurate.

At the end of 1919 Bulgakov was present during heavy fighting between the Whites and separatist forces from the Caucasus region, and he probably suffered an injury in November 1919 during a skirmish at Shali-Aul, which he described in his *Unusual Adventures of a Doctor* (1922). But this was also a moment when he began to take decisive steps away from medicine in order to fulfil his long-cherished vocation as a writer:

One night in 1919, in the depths of autumn, as I was travelling in a dilapidated train, and by the light of a small candle stuck into a kerosene bottle, I wrote my first brief story. In the town to which the train was hauling me, I took the story to the editorial board of a newspaper. And there it was published.[20]

These tentative first steps were consolidated early in 1920, when he joined a group of writers in Vladikavkaz, led by the writer Yury Slyozkin, to launch a journal called *The Caucasus*: 'On 15 February 1920 I experienced a spiritual turning-point, when I abandoned medicine forever, and decided to devote myself to literature.'[21] The journal proved to be short-lived, but in any case political events once more supervened to determine the further course of his life. News was coming in of a recent disastrous defeat of the Whites' elite Cossack troops, and of the advance of the Red Army. And at this critical moment, as the Whites were preparing to withdraw further southwards, Bulgakov undertook a trip to the nearby town of Pyatigorsk, and brought back a louse in his clothing, which infected him with typhus. He became very ill and spent six weeks in bed, tended by Tasya: and when he recovered it was to discover that the White forces had long ago vanished, and that Vladikavkaz had been taken over by the Bolsheviks. He was now trapped in Soviet Russia.

In the spring of 1920, as Bulgakov gradually regained his strength, he was apprehensive that his past as a medical officer and as a journalist for the Whites might be held against him. But although he had one or two unpleasant moments, he was fortunate that his friend Yury Slyozkin had been appointed to run the local department of culture on behalf of the new People's Commissariat of Education, and Bulgakov was taken on there as well. Vladikavkaz's cultural life was surprisingly lively at this time, and a number of well-known writers and theatre directors passed through the town. At first Bulgakov played a role as a public speaker, introducing theatrical performances or literary debates. His first experience of Soviet cultural institutions (the literary and theatrical branches of which were usually known by their acronyms of LITO or TEO) is entertainingly recounted in his *Cuff Notes*, published in 1922–4, but based on the notebooks he had kept during 1920–21. This job went reasonably well, until in October 1920 he decided to speak out after a literary debate about the great national poet of the early nineteenth century, Aleksandr Pushkin, who had been denounced by the iconoclastic young Bolshevik critics. They accused Pushkin of being a servile, hypocritical and pseudo-revolutionary poet and author of bawdy verses, whose works should be consigned to the stove. In this the local hotheads were of course emulating the Futurist manifestos of the day, including the notorious 1912 *Slap in the Face of Public Taste*, in which it had been proposed that 'Pushkin, Tolstoy and Dostoevsky should be thrown overboard from the steamship of modernity'.[22] Bulgakov spoke out in Pushkin's defence, and was satisfied that he had won the battle of words: but after subsequent accusations in the local press that he was a typical bourgeois gent and a wolf in sheep's clothing, he was summarily sacked from his posts (I, 186–92).

However, Bulgakov had been taking steps in a new direction, which perhaps held more promise for the future. June 1920 had seen the staging of his play *Self-defence*, a one-act humoresque set in a modern-day provincial town. And in October, just one week before the disastrous Pushkin evening, the premiere was held of his four-act drama *The Turbin Brothers*. Unfortunately, neither of these early texts has survived, but clearly the latter play was of considerable significance for his later project about the Turbin family, *The White Guard*. In this work, as in the novel, the main protagonist was called Aleksei Turbin (the surname had in fact been a family name on Bulgakov's mother's side). The events depicted in the play, however, were apparently not the same as in the novel, but instead revolved around the 1905 Revolution in Russia, rather than the very recent events of 1918–19. On 1 February 1921 Bulgakov wrote to his cousin Konstantin (Kostya), thanking him for sending him news at last of the rest of the family, and describing how he had submitted both of his plays, together with another one about the Paris commune, to Moscow for consideration by the state theatrical organization (TEO) there. The Moscow TEO was run by the distinguished avant-garde theatre director Vsevolod Meyerkhol'd. Bulgakov had just heard that all three plays had been rejected:

That's an important and fully deserved lesson for me: don't send things which have not been polished!

My life is a torment. Ah, Kostya, you cannot imagine how I would have liked you to be here when *The Turbins* was performed for the first time. You cannot imagine the deep sorrow I felt that the play was being put on in the back of beyond, and that I am four years late with what I should have begun to do long ago – writing.

... When I was called up on stage after the second act I came out with a troubled heart ... And thought, 'But this is my dream come true ... but in what a distorted way: instead of the Moscow stage, a provincial theatre, and instead of the drama about Alyosha [Aleksei] Turbin, the thought of which I had been cherishing, a hastily done, immature thing.'

... At night I sometimes read over the stories I've published previously (in newspapers! in newspapers!), and I think: where is my volume of collected works? Where is my reputation? Where are the wasted years?[23]

Programme for Bulgakov's first play about the Turbin family (Vladikavkaz, 1921).

During this period in Vladikavkaz, Bulgakov wrote two other plays, *The Bridegrooms of Clay* (a 'comedy-bouffe' that he considered one of his best, but which was the only play of this period not to be staged) and *The Sons of the Mullah*, a work he composed together with a lawyer acquaintance who provided him with local colour, and which he described as having been composed in seven days, and being utterly lacking in talent. Only the text of this last play has survived.

In that same letter to Kostya of February 1921, however, Bulgakov mentions two other items of interest. The first is that he has embarked upon writing a novel, 'the only fully considered thing during all this time'. This is the first intimation we have that his obsessive preoccupation with his recent experiences in Kiev, soon to be explored in a range of short stories, will ultimately be transformed into a full-scale work, the novel *The White Guard*. Things were clearly at a fairly tentative stage, however, since in June it turned out that he was refashioning the Turbins' story into a new full-scale drama instead.[24] The other matter he mentions is that he is planning to leave Vladikavkaz in the spring or summer: 'Where am I going? It's possible, but very unlikely, that I will pass through Moscow this summer. I am hoping to travel far . . .'.[25] By April 1921 he asked his sister Nadya to collect together the texts of his early stories and the plays which had been rejected in Moscow, and to burn them in the stove 'supposing that I travel far away and for a long time'. In a further letter to her he adds that she is not to mention any 'medical' matters to his acquaintance from Vladikavkaz.[26] At the end of May, he informed Nadya that he was leaving for Tiflis (Tbilisi), and that Tasya was staying on in Vladikavkaz: 'If Tasya turns up in Moscow, please don't deny her a family welcome, and some advice at first as she establishes her affairs'.[27] All of these cryptic remarks can only be interpreted to mean that he was still apprehensive that his past as a doctor in the White Army would be discovered; that he was planning to leave the country in the foreseeable future; and that he and Tasya were probably going to split up, and he would leave her behind.

However, their marriage was destined to last a little bit longer. By early June, Bulgakov had decided to summon Tasya to join him in Tiflis after all, and a month later they travelled onwards to Batum, a port on the Black Sea coast of Georgia.[28] He still had some money in his pocket after selling their only remaining valuables – their beautiful inscribed wedding rings from 1913. This was his opportunity to try to persuade some sea captain to smuggle him on board and enable his escape from Bolshevik Russia into emigration, where the thought of France, and Paris, was very alluring. But their efforts came to nothing. Bulgakov then despatched Tasya to Moscow, while he made one final attempt to leave – he even sold his overcoat – but in vain. In the late summer of 1921 Bulgakov abandoned the idea of emigration, went to visit his mother in Kiev and travelled on to Moscow to seek his fortune as a writer in Soviet Russia.

2

Moscow, 1921–6

Bulgakov's decision in the late summer of 1921 to abandon his attempt to emigrate represents a momentous choice in his life. His middle-class upbringing, his innate social conservatism and the political stance of indignant hostility to Bolshevism he had expressed in his 1919 article 'Prospects for the Future', had all made things difficult and even dangerous for him after he found himself marooned in the Caucasus as the Red Army took over in 1920. On the other hand, his renewed conviction that literature was the right career for him, rather than medicine, had begun to make life in emigration a less appealing prospect: many Russian writers would indeed find that making a living abroad was extremely difficult, because their potential readership was so small, and some would eventually have to resort to the alternative occupations of Russian émigrés in Paris – taxi-driving or playing the balalaika. His choice was also dictated by practicalities: he had simply been unlucky in his attempts to find a sea captain willing to smuggle him abroad, and he had now run out of money.

However, political developments within Lenin's Russia must also have influenced his thinking about the issue. After seven long years of turmoil encompassing the First World War and both revolutions of 1917, the country's civil war was petering out by 1921, bringing peace at last for the Russian people. But this had been achieved at a terrible economic cost: as well as the massive social disruption and the loss of human lives, the country's agriculture, trade and industry were wrecked. In these circumstances, Lenin had famously made the decision to take one step back in order to jump two steps forward, and in March 1921 he announced the introduction of a New Economic Policy (NEP). Designed to kick-start the economy of the nascent socialist state into life, these measures permitted private enterprise to be reintroduced in areas such as food production and small-scale trade, while the major branches of the economy remained under the control of the state. These NEP measures, which remained in place from 1921 until 1928/9, were largely successful in fulfilling Lenin's purpose of helping the country to get back on its feet. But their character, seemingly so much at odds with the socialist goal of nationalization of all property, lent a flavour of contradiction to all the years of NEP: developments in everyday economic and social life seemed, confusingly, to be running in a direction that was contrary to the professed aims of the Bolshevik Revolution.

These events had a significant impact on the cultural and literary life of the country as well. During these years a whole range of new publishing outlets in the form of publishing houses and journals opened up, some of them with private as opposed to state funding; and the NEP period is also one of relative liberalism as far as censorship laws were concerned. It is not difficult to understand that Bulgakov, who was weighing up his choices during the summer of 1921, may well have been influenced by the recent and startling news from Moscow about NEP to feel that on balance he would be better off staying behind in Russia rather than leaving. With the benefit of hindsight we can see why this was a decision he would come to regret, but he would not be the only person at the time to feel – and to hope – that the worst was now over, and that intellectuals like himself might well be able to establish a modus vivendi in Lenin's Russia.

He therefore left Batum on the Black Sea and headed for the capital, Moscow, to seek his literary fortune in a city in which he had never previously lived. On the way he stopped off in Kiev to

Mikhail's sister Nadezhda (Nadya), 1912.

spend the third week of September 1921 visiting his family, most of whom he had not seen for nearly two years. There was still no news at all of Kolya and Vanya; Varya with her husband Karum had been living in the Crimea, as had Vera; and Nadya was with her husband Andrei in Moscow. Only Lyolya was still at home with their mother. But as life became more settled during 1921, some of the siblings managed to get back to Kiev. As Nadya put it in her diary, written in Bucha that August:

All of us had lived through many serious, even frightening things, and had looked into the face of life and death itself. All of us had grown older and become more serious, all of us had learned to take on serious work, and to do all sorts of things which we had never even concerned ourselves with previously . . . It is good that there is now again the possibility of spending time together, and despite everything, in true Bulgakov fashion we can talk together, too much and loudly, perhaps quarrel, or argue terribly, weep a little and above all laugh our fill and 'fool around' as we tell each other about the most serious things and try to hammer out the most vital questions in our shared lives.[1]

Nadya took pleasure in this return to the hubbub of family life, as when they were younger. Bulgakov himself, writing later to his mother from Moscow, dwelt upon a different pleasure he had enjoyed on his visit:

Can you guess what the most pleasant memory of recent times is for me? How I slept on the divan when I was with you, and drank tea with French buns. I would give a great deal to lie again for a couple of days like that, drinking my fill of tea, without thinking about anything.[2]

It was fortunate that he had managed to make an opportunity to see his mother that autumn, since it turned out to be the last time he ever saw her alive. Varvara Bulgakova's sudden death occurred the following year, at the beginning of February. As far as her peace of mind was concerned, it was fortunate, too, that shortly before her death she received the first news of her other two sons. Kolya's letter of mid-January 1922 from Zagreb told the family that he was studying medicine there. He described his ordered routine and seemed content, although he was feeling the separation from home and family very painfully; and he was able to report that Vanya was also well. Varvara wrote back immediately, of course, but died before Kolya's next letter arrived. Bulgakov was sorely grieved by the loss of his mother, although he could not afford to travel back to Kiev for the funeral.[3] In the opening pages of his novel *The White Guard*, written in the immediate aftermath of this bereavement, there is a very loving evocation of the recently deceased mother as a source of strength and brightness. Bulgakov would repeatedly enjoin his siblings over the next year or two to create a family home in Kiev around their stepfather Ivan Voskresensky, and to live together 'in friendship' – a sentiment that also appears in the novel as the mother's dying request to her children.

Tasya, having been sent away from Batum by Bulgakov, had already been living in Moscow for several weeks, wholly uncertain as to whether she would ever see him again, and whether their marriage was in fact over. Nadya's husband Andrei was keeping an eye on her, but Nadya's letters to Andrei letting him know that Bulgakov was setting off to join Tasya took longer to reach Moscow than he did himself, so the couple's reunion in Moscow at the end of September 1921 came as something of a surprise to Tasya. Shortly afterwards, Andrei went back to Kiev to rejoin Nadya, and the newly reunited Bulgakovs moved into the room Andrei had been occupying in flat 50 at 10 Bol'shaya Sadovaya Street. Their early life together in Moscow was one of extreme hardship: the exceptionally cold winter of 1921–2 meant that issues such as obtaining firewood, or getting hold of decent footwear or a warm enough coat loomed large in their lives, while finding a range of jobs that would bring in an adequate income at a time of runaway inflation consumed all Bulgakov's energy. As he reported to his family, if an income of 3 million roubles a month turned out to be just about adequate to live on in December 1921, by March 1922, 40 million was an absolute minimum. Tasya was in poor health and was unable to work, but Bulgakov told his mother that she was proving a great support to him, taking on all the household tasks she could physically manage: 'You wouldn't believe how domesticated we have become. We conserve every piece of firewood.'[4]

The room they had moved into was in a communal apartment, that characteristic Soviet solution to the housing crisis, which involved formerly spacious private apartments being turned over to multiple occupancy by numerous families, each of them living in a single room and sharing bathroom and kitchen facilities. The contrast with the comfortable family apartment on Andreevsky Hill in Kiev could not have been greater. The inevitable tensions and frictions of shared accommodation were compounded for Bulgakov by the housing committee's regular attempts to evict them, on the grounds that he and Tasya were not formally registered to live there. In the end, Bulgakov appealed for help from the person who was in charge of one of the literary organizations he was working for at the time, who just happened to be Nadezhda Krupskaya, Lenin's wife. A swift intervention from her put a stop to any further harassment.[5] This was an early instance of Bulgakov having the remarkable opportunity of turning to the highest authorities in the land to help him to resolve his personal difficulties. The various neighbours they had to put up with included heavy drinkers, aggressive and quarrelsome families, and prostitutes (Tasya recalled being woken up more than once by hopeful knocks on their door, and having to call out 'she's next door!'). Although it provided him with good material for countless humorous newspaper sketches that he published during his first two or three years in Moscow, and which provided him with his basic income, Bulgakov detested life at Bol'shaya Sadovaya Street. This makes it all the more ironic that these days it has become the main place of pilgrimage for Bulgakov fans in modern Moscow, who come to pay tribute to their favourite cult author by covering the entrance hall and stairway of the apartment block with graffiti.

There is no need to enumerate the numerous, often short-lived publications Bulgakov wrote for in these early years in Moscow, and many of the sketches he produced at the time are of ephemeral interest. One of his first significant jobs, however, may have come his way through a reference he obtained as a result of his involvement in those Soviet literary organizations in Vladikavkaz. In the second part of his autobiographical *Cuff Notes* he gives a very entertaining account of how he came to be offered the job of secretary to the Moscow LITO organization, which was apparently responsible for most literary activities in the capital, even though it consisted of just three members of staff. This post, which he obtained shortly after his arrival, only really lasted for a couple of months, but it gave him a glimpse of the chaotic absurdities of the emergent Soviet bureaucracy, as well as a few first encounters with leading literary figures. Looking further ahead, another of his subsequent jobs that consolidated his standing in Moscow literary life was his commitment to the railway workers' newspaper *The Hooter*, for which he wrote regular humorous sketches (the Russians use the French term *feuilletons*). When he obtained this job in the autumn of 1922 it provided 200 million roubles a month,[6] and he would continue to write for them through 1924 and 1925, and right up until the summer of 1926. In many of these sketches, which he would later describe as 'hateful work',[7] he took semi-literate letters sent in to the newspaper by railway workers, and transformed them into comical anecdotes. Bulgakov described how he became increasingly confident in despatching this task:

> I will let you into another secret here: the composition of a 75–100 line feuilleton would take me, if you include the smoking and the whistling, from 18 to 22 minutes. Getting it typed out, if you include here a little giggling with the typist – 8 minutes. In other words, the whole thing was done in half-an-hour.[8]

His work for *The Hooter* also introduced him to a number of other young writers who had come to Moscow to make a literary career, such as Valentin Kataev, Yury Olesha, the writing duo of Il'f and Petrov, and Mikhail Zoshchenko. Many of these writers, for the most part rather younger than Bulgakov himself, would go on to become some of the most popular comic writers of the NEP era. This kind of work – the rapid creation of compact, witty sketches for the newspapers – was also the way in which Bulgakov's predecessor Anton Chekhov had begun his writing career as he turned away from medicine in the 1880s, and clearly provided a useful schooling in the methods of pithy and laconic humorous dialogue.

When Bulgakov wrote to his mother in November 1921 to report on how he was getting on in Moscow, he told her that, despite the difficult conditions, he was still determined to pursue his literary ambitions:

> The path that I sketched out for myself while still in Kiev, as regards looking for jobs and pursuing my specialism, turned out to be entirely correct. It is impossible for me to work in any other specialism . . . I am writing all this also with the purpose of showing you in what conditions I have been obliged to fulfil my idée-fixe. And that consists in recreating normality within three years: an apartment, clothes and books. We shall have to see whether I succeed.[9]

The job that really made it possible for him to achieve his goals in those early years, however, was his collaboration with the newspaper called *On the Eve*. This new publication represented an unexpected initiative by the Bolshevik government to reach out to the émigré community, and was published simultaneously in Berlin as well as Moscow as testimony to its supposed purpose of rebuilding bridges with intellectuals who had fled the country in the previous few years. For Bulgakov, who within a week or so of his mother's death had written in his diary for 9 February 1922 that this was 'the blackest period of my life' (VIII, 62), the inauguration of this newspaper in Berlin that March (and in Moscow that July) offered a tempting opportunity to make his mark within Russia, but also among Russian readers abroad. Between June 1922 and June 1924 he published on average one piece a month there, including important texts such as the first part of his *Cuff Notes*, and other autobiographical memoir pieces such as *On the Night of the Second* and *The Red Crown*. The main persona that he adopted for his *On the Eve* sketches, however, was that of a reporter on life in the new Moscow, describing for the benefit of his audience abroad the transformations of life there under the Soviet regime. There is a sense, therefore, in which this was the job that allowed him to refashion himself, and to move away from the preoccupation with war and with Kiev that had so dominated his prose writing hitherto. These texts are full of references to current events and to Moscow streets and landmarks, and on reading them it is difficult to believe that this writer was not in fact a native of his adopted city. One of his talents as a writer of both prose and drama would soon emerge as this actor-like capacity to simulate a whole range of voices. And on the whole, Bulgakov had relatively positive things to report to his compatriots abroad, particularly as NEP got under way and life in the capital seemed to be returning to normal. As someone who had been so distressed by the disruption and chaos of war and civic unrest, he was happy to celebrate any signs of a return to normality. In *The Capital City in my Notebook* (1922) he simply describes how an entire street stops to gawp at the almost-forgotten sight of a little boy calmly walking to school with a satchel on his back (1, 260–61). And in the 1923 story *Forty Times Forty* (a reference to the supposed number of onion-domed churches in Moscow), he notes that signs of progress are beginning to be felt:

> Ah, these were still difficult times. You couldn't be confident about the next day. But all the same I (along with people like me) was no longer eating groats and saccharine. There

was meat for dinner. For the first time in three years I didn't 'receive' boots, but 'purchased' them: and they weren't twice the size of my feet, but just a couple of sizes too big (I, 276).

Elsewhere he commented:

> The conviction on Friedrichstrasse [in émigré Berlin] that Russia is finished is not one that I share, and furthermore: the more I observe the kaleidoscope of Moscow, the more the presentiment is strengthened in me that 'it will all work out', and we will still manage to live quite cheerfully.[10]

These comments are fascinating for revealing a Bulgakov who, having become largely disillusioned with the monarchist White movement, was prepared at this point to give the new regime credit for any positive developments (albeit measured largely in terms of a return to a traditional, 'civilized' way of life). In any case he was clear in his own mind that he didn't really belong on one or the other side of the political divide:

> I ended up between both groups . . . The bourgeois took one look at my suit and chased me into the camp of the proletarians. And the proletarians attempted to evict me from my apartment on the grounds that if I wasn't a pure bourgeois, then in any case I was a surrogate one.[11]

Having himself struggled through the hardships of recent years, he could see how repellent the smug resurgent bourgeoisie of the NEP era could appear, with their household servants, starched tablecloths and their ability to lay their hands on all the luxury foods of the past (see the 1923 story *Moscow Scenes*, I, 283–90). After making the decision to stay behind rather than leave Soviet Russia, Bulgakov had fought hard to get where he was now:

'I discovered in myself an unheard-of, extraordinary energy . . . My body became skinny and sinewy, my heart turned to iron, my eye was keen. I had become hardened.'[12] In the *On the Eve* stories we can read an unmistakable pride in what he has achieved, and in what Moscow is becoming, which we should not mistake for naivety about the risk that his writing might be understood as mere propaganda. In his private diary for 26 October 1923 he comments:

> My instincts as far as people are concerned never deceive me. Never. A group of exceptional bastards is gathering around *On the Eve*. I can congratulate myself for being among them. Oh, things will go roughly for me later on, when I will need to scrape off the mud which has attached itself to my name. But I can say one thing with a conscience which is clear as far as I am concerned. Iron necessity obliged me to publish with them. If it had not been for *On the Eve*, neither *Cuff Notes*, nor many other things would have seen the light of day, in which I have been able to utter truthful words in literature. You would have had to be an exceptional hero to remain silent for four whole years, to remain silent with no hope of opening your mouth in the future. And I, unfortunately, am no hero (VIII, 78).

The theme of the somewhat weak, but understandable compromises that ordinary mortals sometimes make in order to achieve what they perceive as a morally worthwhile goal was one that would come to pervade many of Bulgakov's best-known later works.

The reasons why Bulgakov entered into a compromise of which he was fully aware – associating himself with a publication that was patently an instrument of Bolshevik propaganda in Europe – were twofold. Firstly, he thirsted for a literary reputation, and the journal *On the Eve* was widely read. Secondly, it provided him with a reliable income, while also giving him the time to pursue the much larger project with which he proposed to establish himself in the literary world, his novel *The White Guard*. In his visible, published life as a writer, he became established as a witty reporter of modern-day, Soviet-era Moscow; but during 1922 and 1923 the writing of *The White Guard* became the opportunity for him also to travel back in time and space to conjure up a lyrical, subjective account of the family, the home, the city, the social setting and the political structures which had been irrevocably lost for him over the course of just a few years. Much of the writing was completed during 1922, after the death of his mother, and the whole thing was pretty much finished by the end of August 1923. A couple of days later, he confided to his diary his conviction that he had accomplished something genuinely important:

> In the midst of my spleen and my yearning for the past, occasionally, as at present in this absurd situation of short-term overcrowding, in this repellent room, in this repellent apartment, I experience surges of confidence and strength. At this moment too I sense my thoughts surging upwards, I sense that it is the truth that I am immeasurably stronger as a writer than any of those whom I know.[13]

Altogether, Bulgakov had shown himself to be a shrewd tactician during 1921–3: having arrived in Moscow as a completely unknown writer from the provinces, he and Tasya had first established themselves with a modest place to live, and had then managed between them to keep fed and clothed. He had shown initiative and determination in making himself known in literary circles, initially through some administrative roles, and through his steady stream of small-scale topical pieces of fictional writing, which soon began to attract attention within Russia and then abroad as well. By the summer of 1923 he was negotiating for the publication of more substantial pieces in *On the Eve* such

as *Cuff Notes*, and of a new story, *Diaboliada*, a Gogolian tale in
which an office worker in a match factory is driven to insanity
by a manager with an apparent double. The story appeared
in February 1924 in the journal *Nedra* (The Depths) and was
then reprinted in a volume of his stories published under the
same title, *Diaboliada*, in 1925. This was the only book he ever
published in his lifetime. The story was lauded for its cinematic
structure and for its blend of the fantastic and the everyday by the
distinguished Leningrad writer Yevgeny Zamyatin, who would
soon become a close friend. And at the same time Bulgakov had
found the energy to write his first novel. That autumn he gave his
first complete reading of *The White Guard* (in four sessions) to the
Green Lamp literary society. By the time distinguished émigré
writers such as Aleksei Tolstoy returned to Russia in 1923, seduced
by the Soviet government's conciliatory gestures, Bulgakov's
reputation had already become something to be reckoned with.

Among the returning émigrés was a lively and attractive young
woman called Lyubov' Yevgen'evna Belozerskaya (1895–1987), who
had travelled to Constantinople and then lived in Paris and Berlin,
which lent her an air of considerable sophistication. At the time she
first met the Bulgakovs, at a party for Aleksei Tolstoy early in 1924,
her marriage to a journalist from *On the Eve* had recently ended.
She was amused by the ridiculous yellow patent-leather shoes
Bulgakov was wearing (given the difficulty he had had in obtaining
them, he was rather indignant at this). Her first impression of him
was of a man of 30 to 32, with blond hair smoothly combed, and
a slanting parting. He had blue eyes and irregular features, his
nostrils were sharply delineated, and he furrowed his brow when
he spoke: but overall she felt that it was an attractive face, and he
rather reminded her of Chaliapin.[14] Soon they began seeing each
other, and the long-suffering Tasya was informed by Bulgakov in
the spring of 1924 that he intended to leave her, although it took
until November that year for him finally to move out to live with

Lyubov'
Belozerskaya
(Lyuba).

Lyubov' (Lyuba). As Bulgakov rose in society towards a more glamorous life among the literary elite of the capital, his first wife no longer seemed to fit in. Tasya was particularly wounded when she saw the journal publication of the first part of *The White Guard* in December 1925, and discovered that he had dedicated this novel describing their shared past to his new love. Bulgakov continued to concern himself with Tasya's material welfare, but to the end of his life confessed to a feeling of guilt about the way he had treated her. His second marriage took place on 30 April 1925.[15]

Lyuba was a charming, fun-loving, independent person, with many connections in the Moscow intelligentsia. She was also very confident, and during the seven and a half years of her marriage to Bulgakov she undertook relatively unusual activities for a woman at the time, such as horse riding and gaining a driving licence. Bulgakov found her physically bewitching (in his private diary for December 1925 he observes ruefully how captivated he is by her).[16] There was a lot of laughter and playfulness: in her memoirs, Lyuba's account of their marriage is full of stories about the special comic words and phrases they used, their nicknames for each other and for their friends (Bulgakov became known at this time as 'Maka', from a children's rhyme), the outings with friends to go skiing or play tennis, the parties, charades and practical jokes.

One of the first new pieces he wrote while he was living with Lyuba was his brilliant novella *The Heart of a Dog* (January–March 1925). In this comical yet profound story, a stray dog, Sharik, is taken in by a Professor Preobrazhensky, who fattens him up and then uses him for a surgical experiment in which his pituitary gland and testicles are removed and replaced with those of a recently deceased proletarian drunk. To the professor's astonishment the creature survives the operation, and then goes on to develop into an obnoxious humanoid with all the dissolute vices of the original human donor. Under the influence of the local Bolshevik party activists, he also becomes an insufferable critic of Preobrazhensky's entire lifestyle. Unable to bear his disruptive presence any longer, the professor feels compelled to reverse the operation, and the creature gradually turns back into the endearing mongrel of the story's opening. The story explores the ethics of medical experimentation, eugenics and indeed sexual therapies, and the professor remains a troubling and ambiguous figure. At the same time, however, the Party activists of the building's housing committee are presented as both stupid and cynical. Some commentators have seen the story as a bold political allegory, warning against the dangers of social experiments such as those undertaken by Lenin in accelerating the revolutionary process predicted by Marx, in order to rush towards the creation of a new Soviet man, *Homo sovieticus*. Bulgakov had already touched upon similar themes in a story written three months earlier, *The Fateful Eggs*, in which another scientist's experiments meddling with the natural order of things go catastrophically wrong when the state takes over control of the process he is investigating, and the country is nearly destroyed by monstrous creatures. Like many other NEP writers of a similar background to his own, Bulgakov insists that man is atavistically inclined to remain true to his essential nature, and that the social revolution which Socialism was supposed to usher in still has a very long way to go.

The Heart of a Dog also has surprisingly dramatic qualities for a work of prose. As in his other prose works, Bulgakov concentrates on giving his protagonists their own strongly defined voices: the opening pages of *The Heart of a Dog* are delightfully narrated by the dog Sharik, who gives an improbably knowing, shrewd account of the reality of Soviet hierarchies under the new regime (he remembers the good old cook at Count Tolstoy's who used to feed the dogs scraps, unlike the modern-day proletarian chef who has cruelly scalded him; and he can give a precise account of the sexual proclivities of a newly powerful proletarian official). The narrative perspective in the novella varies, and the professor's loyal assistant Bormental' offers another subjective viewpoint in the diary entries he writes, with astonishment and horror breaking through what is supposed to be an impartial scientific record of the experiment. Once again, with characters defined almost entirely through action and language, the text seemed to cry out to be staged: and indeed the Moscow Art Theatre even signed a contract on 2 March 1926 for a stage adaptation – which was then withdrawn for censorship reasons.[17] The moment the text was finally published in the Soviet Union in 1987, theatres rushed to adapt the work for the stage, with three concurrent productions running in Moscow that same summer.

The writing of *The Heart of a Dog* during the first months of 1925 coincided with the partial publication of *The White Guard* in a planned three-part serialization by an enterprising editor, Isay Lezhnyov, in his journal *Rossiya* (Russia).[18] However, it was always going to be a risky undertaking to publish a book with such an inflammatory title, especially since its sympathies were so blatantly in favour of the now officially reviled Russian middle class. Before the third and final part could be published, the journal was closed down by the Soviet authorities and Lezhnyov was arrested and forced to leave the country shortly afterwards. This was the only portion of the book to appear in print in the Soviet Union for several decades. Long after its author's death it was finally permitted in the Thaw period and published in 1966. This makes it all the more remarkable that an incomplete publication of this kind should have had such a huge influence on its author's reputation.

The explanation for this phenomenon is that a sharp-eyed literary consultant at the Moscow Art Theatre had spotted the novel in Lezhnyov's *Russia* and recognized the text's theatrical potential. We might remember that Bulgakov's investigation of his family's history had initially found expression in dramatic form (the play *The Turbin Brothers*, written in Vladikavkaz, and later burnt). He had then revisited the subject in writing the novel *The White Guard*: but in fact, even before the approach from the Moscow Art Theatre, Bulgakov had already started work on his own dramatization of the text. The dream of establishing himself as a playwright had never left him, and the invitation that arrived in the spring of 1925 from the Moscow Art Theatre, the most famous theatre of the day, to develop his novel into a play for them, would inaugurate his success in fulfilling his most cherished ambition.

What attracted the renowned theatre to the project? Above all it was the dearth of 'new' drama of a quality that would attract audiences, while at the same time providing urgently needed evidence to the Soviet authorities that the Art Theatre was not exclusively tied to its 'reactionary', pre-Revolutionary repertory. The novel's subject-matter would undoubtedly be controversial,

but in the atmosphere of relaxation under NEP the directors of
the theatre, Konstantin Stanislavsky and Vladimir Nemirovich-
Danchenko, felt that it was on balance a risk worth taking. In the
event, they only just got away with it. Under the title *The Days of the
Turbins*, Bulgakov's adaptation of *The White Guard* was premiered
at the Moscow Art Theatre on 10 October 1926, and secured the
aspiring dramatist's reputation as one of the most exciting and
controversial writers of his generation, a Chekhov for the Soviet era.

In one episode from his later *Theatrical Novel*, a project he
embarked upon towards the very end of his life, Bulgakov recreated
for us through his blatantly autobiographical writer-hero Maksudov
a fascinating glimpse of how the project of turning his novel into a
play may have come about. It began – we are not surprised to learn
– with dreams, which were populated by figures from his life in
Kiev six years earlier, and which by now seemed almost like part
of another world:

These people were born in my dreams, and then they stepped
out of my dreams and established themselves very firmly in my
garret. It was clear that I was not going to be able to part from
them. But what was I to do with them? At first I just chatted to

Bulgakov (front row, centre) with the cast of *The Days of the Turbins*, 5 October 1926.

them, but all the same I was obliged to take the manuscript of my novel out of the drawer. And after that it began to seem to me in the evenings that something full of colours was emerging from the white page. When I looked closely, screwing up my eyes, I realized that it was a picture. And what's more, the picture was not flat, but three-dimensional. It was like a small box, and between the lines of text you could see inside it: the lights were on, and the same little figures were moving about in it as I had described in the novel . . . As time went on sounds could be heard from the chamber inside the book. I could distinctly hear the sound of a piano . . . I could act out my entire life by playing this game, gazing at the page . . . But how was I to capture these little figures? In such a way that they would not ever leave again? And one night I decided to describe this magical chamber . . . I can see that it is evening, the light is on. The fringe of the lampshade. There is a score open on the piano. They're playing Gounod's *Faust*. Suddenly *Faust* falls silent, but a guitar starts up. Who's playing? Here he is, coming through the door with a guitar in his arms. And I can hear him singing the refrain. So I write: he sings the refrain. This turns out to be a delightful game! . . . I occupied myself for three nights or so, playing around with this first picture, and towards the end of the last night I understood that I was writing a play (I, 451–2).

What is revealed in this passage is the closeness of the inter-relationship between the drafting of prose and the creation of drama, as well as the importance writing had for him as a means of undertaking an imaginative journey into presently inaccessible times and places. Drama becomes a private means of holding on to a vanished past. At the same time, the experience of inspiration is configured in the Romantic tradition as the mimetic reproduction of a wholly realistic vision which comes to him initially in the form of a dream, and is then so fully embodied in the pages of his novel that he can further recreate it as dramatic action, with lighting and sound effects already provided, and within the framework of a proscenium arch. In his *Theatrical Novel* the narrator also conveys to the reader his subsequent delight, once his play has been accepted, at finding himself inside the plush theatre, getting to know all the backstage characters, and sitting in on rehearsals in which actors perform the sheer magic of transformation which is their professional talent. As Bulgakov/Maksudov concludes with a sigh of contentment, 'This world is my world' (I, 455).

The year 1925 may have been when Bulgakov truly established himself in Moscow as a writer and playwright, but it was also the year in which he first came to the attention of the authorities as someone they needed to keep an eye on. His *White Guard* had not perhaps been the only reason they had closed down the journal *Russia*, but the enthusiasm with which his *Heart of a Dog* was greeted when he started to give readings of it in literary circles certainly confirmed the authorities' view of him as a subversive. After he had read the first part on 7 March 1925, one member of his audience compiled a report for the secret police, the OGPU: 'The entire piece is written in tones which are hostile to the Soviet system and exude boundless contempt.' The author argued that Bulgakov had become the most dangerous of writers in Moscow, and urged the censors not to allow the work to be published. This was followed by a further denunciation to the OGPU after the reading of the second part on 21 March, warning of the risk that the text would be seized upon for propaganda purposes by hostile émigrés if it were to be published. Negotiations about a possible publication continued through the spring and summer, but the verdict given that September by Lev Kamenev, a Party leader who had been thought to be a liberal, was final: 'This is a sharp pamphlet about the modern age, and it should under no circumstances be published.'[19]

On 7 May 1926 the OGPU issued an explicit warning to Bulgakov by turning up at his flat and confiscating papers, principally two typed copies of *The Heart of a Dog* and some volumes of private diaries intermittently covering the years 1921–5. There is some uncertainty about what happened subsequently. Bulgakov was evidently not that intimidated, since he appealed to the influential writer Maksim Gor'ky to intervene on his behalf to have the materials returned to him. Lyuba states in her memoirs that this took place two years later, but there is some evidence that it took at least until 1930 before he received them back from the OGPU.[20] In any case Bulgakov resolved never to keep a private diary again.

The next thing was that Bulgakov was summoned for interrogation by the OGPU. This was on 22 September 1926, just one day before Party officials were due to attend a run-through of *The Days of the Turbins* at the Moscow Art Theatre. A transcript of the interrogation has survived, and shows that Bulgakov conducted himself with considerable confidence and frankness. He gave a full and largely accurate account of his history:

> I began to engage in literary work from the autumn of 1919 in the town of Vladikavkaz, under the Whites. I wrote some brief stories and sketches for the White press. In my works I expressed a critical and hostile attitude to Soviet Russia . . . My sympathies were entirely on the side of the Whites, whose retreat I observed with dismay and bewilderment. At the moment when the Red Army took over I was in Vladikavkaz, ill with recurrent typhus. When I recovered I began to work with the Soviet authorities, running LITO for the Commissariat of Education.

To a question about his Party affiliation and political convictions, he replied that he belonged to no party, adding:

> I have been tied with too strong roots to Soviet Russia as it was being constructed to be able to imagine how I could exist

as a writer outside it. I consider the Soviet system to be exceptionally solid. I can see a whole mass of flaws in everyday life today, and thanks to my temperament, I take a satirical position in this respect and reflect that in my works.

He also commented on *The Heart of a Dog*, which now had no prospect of getting published, and acknowledged, in response to a direct question, that there was a political level to the story that was in opposition to the existing system:

I consider that the story *Heart of a Dog* turned out to be much more topical than I had supposed when I was composing it, and I understand the reasons for it being banned for publication . . . I have more than once received invitations to read this work in various places, and have turned them down, since I understood that I had gone over the top in the maliciousness of my satire, and that the story was provoking too much attention.

He provided information about how many people had attended the readings he had given, though he refused on ethical grounds to list their names. Bulgakov concluded by commenting on what seems to have been a suggestion by his interrogator that he should write about the favoured topics for writers at the time:

I cannot write about peasant themes, since I don't like the countryside . . . It is difficult for me to write about the everyday lives of workers, even though I know about that much more than peasant life, but even so I don't know it very well. And indeed I'm not very interested in it, for the following reason: I am absorbed and keenly interested in the everyday life of the Russian intelligentsia, and I love it: I consider it to be a very important component of our country, even if it is weak. Its fate is close to my heart, and its experiences are precious to me. That means I am only capable of writing about the life of the intelligentsia in the Soviet state. But I have a satirical mindset. Things come from my pen which occasionally, as it seems, cause a sharp reaction in Communist circles of society. I always write with a clear conscience, and I write as I see things. The negative aspects of life in the Soviet state attract my constant attention, because I instinctively find a great deal of material there for myself: I am a satirist.[21]

As Varlamov puts it, this interrogation served a dual function: taking place on the day before the dress rehearsal attended by members of the government and of the censorship organs, it was clearly a warning that with *The Heart of a Dog* he had gone a step too far. And yet at the same time, the fact that he got through the occasion by speaking the truth, and that *The Days of the Turbins* did go on to be staged, indicated that he had passed some kind of test and had been granted the freedom to continue writing – at least for the time being – by the secret police and Party leaders.

3

Four Plays, 1926–9

The presence of representatives of the highest echelons of the Communist Party alongside members of the State Repertory Committee (the board of censors) at the Moscow Art Theatre's dress rehearsal of *The Days of the Turbins* on 23 September 1926 might seem to us astonishing. But the Bolsheviks had taken an inordinate interest in literature and theatre from the earliest days of Soviet power. Throughout the 1920s and '30s it was not uncommon for novels or plays – as well as the fates of their authors – to be discussed at length during full meetings of the Politburo of the Communist Party (whose role and size was largely comparable to that of a British cabinet). This model of relations between rulers and artists in Russia dated back to exactly a century earlier, when Tsar Nicholas I had appointed himself Aleksandr Pushkin's personal censor in 1826. Every new work thereafter by Russia's leading poet had to be submitted to the chief of police, Count Benkendorf, who then consulted with leading conservative critics of the day before delivering the work to the tsar for his final scrutiny and comment. It was Nicholas I who personally advised Pushkin to rewrite his historical verse play *Boris Godunov* as a novel 'à la Walter Scott', and who deleted words and lines from his great poem *The Bronze Horseman*, which the tsar felt to be offensive to the institution of monarchy. In the Soviet era, the Bolsheviks continued this tradition, and Stalin seems increasingly to have felt that making similar personal interventions in literary and theatrical affairs was a way of proceeding that could only add lustre to his personal reputation, indicating that he, no less than any tsar, was capable of becoming the ultimate arbiter of Russian culture.

This, then, was one of the major challenges that Bulgakov faced as he began to reach full maturity as a dramatist in the mid-1920s: how to negotiate issues of censorship pressure from the Party and from the Repertory Committee (now the main agency for the increasingly centralized bureaucratic and political control of the theatre), while retaining his integrity with respect to the content of his plays. A second challenge he faced concerned the form and style of his dramatic works in an era of radical experimentation, when in the aftermath of 1917 many avant-garde artists had rushed to identify their work as 'Revolutionary' art. The tension between old and new, traditional and mould-breaking in the world of theatre was exemplified in the contrasting approaches to the staging of drama by Konstantin Stanislavsky of the Moscow Art Theatre and his erstwhile pupil, Vsevolod Meyerkhol'd. Stanislavsky's name was inextricably identified with that of Chekhov, whose plays had captured the 'undramatic' unfolding of everyday middle-class life in the provinces. These had been staged at the turn of the century by the Moscow Art Theatre with extraordinary attention to realistic detail, down to dogs barking, birdsong and steam rising from the samovars. Meyerkhol'd's work, as for example in his 1918 and 1921 stagings of the Futurist Vladimir Mayakovsky's *Mystery-Bouffe*, made an explicit attack on this Stanislavskian tradition: there was to be no more proscenium arch, no passive observation by the audience, no psychological realism, but instead a form of theatre that would fully involve the audience in the proletarian cause, culminating in the shared singing of the Internationale by everyone present. Meyerkhol'd's radical programme was designed to reach out to a new audience of urban workers, using the language of propaganda, sometimes by taking drama out of the theatre itself and on to the streets. Echoing political events, he called his programme 'October in the Theatre'.

Bulgakov, whose first plays written in Vladikavkaz were rejected by Meyerkhol'd's TEO organization in 1921, was intensely aware even at that point that Meyerkhol'd and Mayakovsky represented the dominant theatrical ethos of the day, both in political and in theatrical terms. In an article called 'October in the Theatre' written while he was still living in Vladikavkaz in 1920, he had noted that the three years since the Revolution had already seen a complete change in the social make-up of audiences, and he predicted that the barrier between audience and stage represented by the proscenium arch would shortly be pulled down.[1] This early essay on drama reminds us just how important these issues were to him: it is worth remembering that Bulgakov was known in his own lifetime, and indeed right up until the late 1960s, almost exclusively as a playwright (he was ultimately the author of fourteen plays, stage adaptations and opera librettos). During 1921–6 his literary reputation had been created by his publications of prose; after 1926, and until his death in 1940, he had to rely on the stage to keep his name in the public eye. His projects as a dramatist throughout the 1920s consciously challenged all that Meyerkhol'd and Mayakovsky stood for, sometimes by virtue of the sheer difference of what he was undertaking, and sometimes, as in the case of his play *The Crimson Island* (1926–7), in an explicit polemic with their positions.

After the initial approach from the Moscow Art Theatre, Bulgakov worked swiftly to create the first draft of his play based on *The White Guard*, completing most of the work on it between June and September 1925. But by the autumn a number of problems emerged. Firstly, the initial lengthy version he had created, closely following the structure of the novel, was clearly too cumbersome, and the theatre demanded that it be reworked, which in turn threatened to delay its staging. Then it became apparent that the senior, Chekhov-era actors in the Art Theatre were unhappy that the roles were almost entirely for young people; indeed, the play would prove to be the springboard that launched the careers of an entire new Soviet generation of actors. And that was quite apart from the obvious political issues surrounding the staging of a work that seemed to cherish the values of the social and political class alluded to in the title, the White Guard, who so recently had been the principal enemy of Bolshevism. The author of another secret report to the OGPU on 19 July 1926 commented as follows:

> In literary circles great astonishment is expressed that this play has been allowed through by the Repertory Committee, since it has a distinct and unambiguous White-Guard flavour. According to the opinions of people who have heard the work, one can say that the play is rather powerful as an artistic piece, and with its powerful, vivid scenes has the specific goal of awakening sympathy for the Whites as they battle for their cause . . . Writers who belong to the Soviet camp are talking about the play with indignation . . . As for those in the anti-Soviet camp, then there is great rejoicing at the fact that it has proved possible to negotiate a path for the play through a whole series of 'obstacles'. People are saying this openly.[2]

Bulgakov was nevertheless unhappy about a number of changes the theatre insisted upon: the transformation of the central character of the doctor Aleksei Turbin into an army colonel of the same name was probably a wise decision in dramatic terms, even though it meant amalgamating three of the novel's original characters into one; like Stanislavsky himself, he deeply regretted the Repertory Committee's last-minute insistence upon the excision of the scene in which Petlyura's men torture a Jew; and he only reluctantly agreed to change the original title of *The White Guard*, which was deemed too provocative, and replace it with the rather anodyne *Days of the Turbins*.

Anatoly Smeliansky, the historian of the Moscow Art Theatre, makes fascinating points about the over-long first draft of 1925, emphasizing that some of the features of the play that were lost in its rewriting were precisely those things which in fact marked Bulgakov out as a genuinely original voice in Russian drama. In rationalizing the characters and turning Aleksei into a soldier and leader, a whole dimension of lyricism was lost, and the quality of indeterminacy with which the original novel ends began to be lost sight of. In not following the extraordinary stage directions, where scenes do not simply succeed one another but, as in dreams, vanish into darkness and spring into the light, the project was restored to realism. In other words, the Moscow Art Theatre – for perhaps understandable reasons – seemed determined to turn Bulgakov into another Chekhov.[3]

The dress rehearsal, which took place on 24 June 1926, had been attended by two of the Moscow Art Theatre's fiercest Communist opponents, Vladimir Blyum and Aleksandr Orlinsky. Blyum declared that the play was nothing but an apologia for the White cause, and could not possibly be staged. Orlinsky felt that these bourgeois heroes should be shown in their true relations to their servants and doormen, as exploitative bullies.[4] It took all the theatre's negotiating skills to persuade the Repertory Committee to allow the production to go ahead. Above all, it was felt necessary to strengthen and clarify the political message of the ending, so that the Turbin family and their friends should make quite clear their attitude to the Bolsheviks as they entered and seized the city of Kiev. Aleksei, who in his new role as a colonel is far more decisive than he was in the novel, declares before he is wounded that the White movement is finished, and discourages those who are considering joining the remaining White forces and fighting on: 'They will force you to fight against your own people . . . The people are not with us. They are against us' (II, 488). The brave officer Myshlaevsky concludes that, as a patriot, the best thing is to stay in Russia and see what happens; and the idealist Nikolay, the brightest hope for the future, concludes that this moment represents the prologue to a new era in history.[5] On the morning of the final run-through for the authorities, on 23 September 1926, it was decided that the play should not only end with the strains of the Internationale, accompanying the entry of the Bolsheviks into the city, but that the music should rise to a crescendo at this point.[6] This was an improbably 'orthodox' ending to the play, which precisely brought it into line with all the Bolshevik propaganda works of Mayakovsky and Meyerkhol'd. Arguments continued between the OGPU, the Repertory Committee and the People's Commissariat of Enlightenment (Ministry of Culture), while the Theatre and the author waited to hear what the outcome would be. On 30 September 1926, at a full meeting of the Politburo of the Communist Party of the USSR, it was finally concluded that the play should be permitted, although only for performance at the Moscow Art Theatre, and only for the 1926–7 season.[7]

The Art Theatre's hunch that Bulgakov would write a good play for them proved justified by the particular talents they discovered in him as they worked on the project. Pavel Markov, whose distinguished career as a literary adviser and director at the Moscow Art Theatre would extend from 1923 until the 1960s, identified one key dimension of Bulgakov's character that helped him become so successful:

> In actual fact Bulgakov was himself a wonderful actor. Perhaps it is precisely this quality which in general determines the true essence of a dramatist, for any dramatist – I mean, of course, a good one – is inevitably an actor at heart . . . But there was one paradoxical thing: his appetite as an actor and author could not be satisfied by any single role in a play: what he needed was not just one character, but many characters, not one image, but many images. If you had asked him to perform any play he had written, he would have performed it in its entirety, role after role, and he would have done it with perfect skill. And so it was with *The Days of the Turbins*: he demonstrated almost all the parts

during rehearsals, helping the actors willingly and generously . . .
And he operated not with abstract discussions, but with concrete
images, often by showing things directly himself . . . The actors
grasped that blend of the tragic, the comic and the lyrical which
lent this show its special charm.[8]

Stanislavsky endorsed this view of Bulgakov as a consummate man
of the theatre when he wrote in 1930 that Bulgakov had effectively
directed *The Days of the Turbins* himself, 'or at least he provided
those sparkles which glittered and made the success of the entire
show'.[9] Bulgakov's family and friends would also have recognized
this quality in him of utter immersion in the dramatic. Lyuba
described him walking around his study as he dictated texts to
her, acting one part and then another as he went along: 'It was a
very entertaining performance.'[10] One friend, Sergey Yermolinsky,
remembered how he composed opera libretti in the 1930s, playing
one after another the parts of opera singer, composer, orchestra
and conductor, as well as prancing around the room in his dressing-
gown performing the dances.[11] The writer Konstantin Paustovsky
commented:

> When you talked to Bulgakov you were left with the impres-
> sion that to start with he even 'acted out' his prose works. He
> was capable of representing any character from his stories
> and novels with unusual expressiveness. He had seen them,
> he had heard them, he knew them through and through. It
> seemed as though he had lived alongside them his whole life.[12]

All these memoirists concurred about his mercurial talent for
switching voices. Furthermore, the boundaries between real life
and the dramatic were far from rigid for him: not only did he pour
his lived experiences into theatre, but he theatricalized his past and
present lives. Sometimes he did this just for the sheer pleasure of

it; his third wife, Yelena, recalled how he loved to visit restaurants, simply so as to observe the other diners:

> He would sit down and say: 'Have a look at that table. There are four people sitting there. Would you like me to tell you what their relationships are, what their jobs are, what they're talking about, and what is tormenting them?' Maybe he just improvised it all and made it up, but when I looked at those people it seemed to me that this was how it must be, so convincing were his arguments.[13]

Increasingly, however, the writing of drama would also provide him with an avenue of escape from the here and now into a realm of unconstrained self-expression, in defiance of the ever-more oppressive censorship.

Despite the blatantly pro-Bolshevik transformations of Bulgakov's original concept, the production was still perceived by critics from the Communist camp as a profoundly reactionary work, an impression that was reinforced by the traditional, realist staging of the work. As Markov put it, '*The Days of the Turbins* became in its own way a new *Seagull* for the Moscow Arts Theatre.'[14] Bulgakov's reputation in the press was immediately established as that of an apparent conservative, both in political and theatrical terms. And after the production had provoked fierce attacks in the Communist press, Bulgakov responded quirkily by taking steps to alter his appearance: he started combing his hair more neatly and took to wearing starched collars – at one stage he even had a photograph taken of himself wearing a monocle – in order to present himself provocatively in an old-fashioned, conservative guise.[15]

Meanwhile, the public flocked to the production, and there were scenes of hysteria in the auditorium as audience members cried out or swooned with emotion at this vivid re-creation of a social trauma so many of them had only recently endured. An ambulance was

Bulgakov with his provocative monocle, 1926.

stationed outside the theatre for every performance.[16] Lyuba
recalled an occasion when one completely absorbed woman in the
audience called out in agitation to the actors to let someone in when
he knocked: 'Come on, open up! He's one of us!'[17] A further OGPU

report dated 18 October 1926 stated: 'All of Moscow's intelligentsia are talking about *The Days of the Turbins* . . . It's become very difficult to get hold of a ticket.'[18] There would be many battles ahead to keep this play on the stage – there were further bans, disagreements at the highest levels, influential interventions, and Politburo discussions of the play when it came to extending its run beyond the summer of 1927 – but in fact it was performed almost a thousand times, providing Bulgakov with one of his most significant sources of regular income for several years.[19] One of the most mysterious aspects of its success was the great regard that Stalin personally had for the play, which he came to watch on as many as fourteen occasions: Stalin's apparent admiration for the work certainly shaped the outcome of several of the Politburo's discussions. Even so, *The Days of the Turbins* could not be published in Bulgakov's lifetime, and it only appeared in print for the first time some thirty years later, in 1955.

Even before *The Days of the Turbins* reached the stage, the Moscow Art Theatre asked Bulgakov to sign a further contract with them, for a stage adaptation of *The Heart of a Dog*: however, that plan had to be abandoned after the OGPU confiscation of the typescript of the story in May 1926. But the Art Theatre was not the only company to have spotted his potential as a playwright. As early as 1925, the Vakhtangov Theatre, another of Moscow's best-known theatres, approached Bulgakov to invite him to write a comedy for them. Bulgakov decided to return to the theme of modern-day Moscow this time. Lyuba recalled that he came across a newspaper cutting about a woman called Zoya, who had run a dressmaking establishment that became a gambling den by night.[20] Bulgakov located the events of his new play, *Zoyka's Apartment*, just down the road from where he had lived with Tasya in the communal apartment on Bol'shaya Sadovaya Street. He combined this real-life anecdote with an idea he had first developed in one of the short pieces that made up the collection *Diaboliada*, called 'A Chinese Story' (1923). This described how a young Chinese immigrant comes to Moscow, meets an older Chinese man who runs a drug den, and ends up fighting for the Red Army, and perishing, without ever having learnt enough Russian to understand what is going on. Once again, as with the writing of the play that became *The Days of the Turbins* on the basis of the novel *The White Guard*, Bulgakov developed a piece of drama from something originally written in prose. His ease in switching between the two genres is anticipated in the subtitle he gave to 'A Chinese Story': 'Six scenes instead of a story'. But when he came to conjure up the creation of the play *Zoyka's Apartment* in his later semi-autobiographical *Theatrical Novel*, it was once again his 'magic box' he described:

> In the evenings a waltz could be heard through the floorboards, one and the same one each time (someone was trying to learn it), and this waltz gave birth to pictures in the little box which were rather strange and harsh. Thus, for example, I imagined that there was an opium den downstairs, and something even began to take shape which I casually called in my own mind 'the third act'. To be precise, there was blue-grey smoke, a woman with an asymmetrical face, some man in a tailcoat who was poisoned by the smoke, and a man with a lemon-coloured face and slanting eyes who was creeping upon him with a Finnish knife. There was a blow from the knife, and a gushing of blood. This was a hallucination, as you can see! Nonsense! And who could I submit such a play to, with a third act like that? (I, 550–51)

Bulgakov was in negotiation with the Vakhtangov Theatre about terms for *Zoyka's Apartment* in September 1925, and he gave a first reading of the play to them on 11 January 1926. In other words, he had two utterly contrasting plays being rehearsed simultaneously during 1926 in two of Moscow's top theatres, despite never having been staged in the city previously. *Zoyka's Apartment* had its official

Scene from Bulgakov's play *Zoyka's Apartment*, 1926–9.

premiere less than three weeks after *The Days of the Turbins*, on 28 October 1926.

In this play for the Vakhtangov Theatre, which was set in 1925, Bulgakov gave a very different impression of Moscow during the NEP era from the optimistic picture he had provided just three to four years previously for the Berlin readers of *On the Eve*. By twisting the corrupt chairman of the residents' committee round her little finger, Zoyka has managed to use her apartment to set up a dressmaking firm. By night this will be transformed into a salon where wealthy patrons will enjoy a risqué fashion show, along with dancing the foxtrot (deeply disapproved of at the time by the Soviet authorities),[21] drinking champagne and flirting with attractive models. Her goal, just like that of her accomplices, is to earn enough money to flee Soviet Russia for the delights of Paris, Nice and Monte Carlo. Even the Chinese drug dealers she works with, whose jealousy over her maidservant leads to murder and the collapse of all their hopes in a police scandal, are also desperate to get out of the USSR and return to their homes in Shanghai. Zoyka's lover, a former count dispossessed by the Revolution, is helplessly addicted to morphine and suffers melancholic longings for his lost past. This is conveyed in the lines he croons from a well-known Rachmaninov romance (based on a Pushkin poem), in which a woman's songs conjure up for the speaker 'Another life and a distant shore . . .'.[22] Not one of these characters lives in the Soviet present; they all travel elsewhere in their dreams and in their hopes. The stage directions requiring instantaneous changes of lighting or setting reinforce our sense of the mystifications and demonic transformations from scene to scene. The amoral world of this NEP-era society has nothing to do with the Communist ideals promulgated by the Party. Instead, it is a world of appearances and masks: the 'respectable' dressmaking business is a cover for the staging of a decadent floor-show; the portrait of Karl Marx that presides over the apartment by day is replaced every evening at closing time by a saucy nude; most of the characters 'dress up' in order to assume false characters; Zoyka's 'administrator' Ametistov has any number of identity cards, ready for all situations; and the cherubic-looking Chinese laundryman is in fact a pitiless murderer. Bulgakov's *White Guard* and *Days of the Turbins* had been dominated by the leitmotif of Valentin's aria from Gounod's *Faust*, evoking feelings of love and honour. But in this play, what prevails is Mephistopheles' satanic aria from the same opera, his song of 'The Golden Calf', frenziedly celebrating man's impious subjection to the power of money.

The Vakhtangov Theatre audiences were very enthusiastic about this fast-moving, sometimes farcical tragedy with its topical subject-matter, and the production was a sell-out in its first season in 1926–7. Over the next couple of years the play would be staged in eight other Soviet cities.[23] But the critics from the Communist establishment were predictably far less keen on the work, and campaigned for it to be banned: some attacked its form, some its vulgar and harmful content, and some denounced Bulgakov himself for his pre-revolutionary, petty-bourgeois mentality.[24] The play was taken off between November 1927 and April 1928, but then allowed back on stage again, reflecting the twists and turns of the public debate about Bulgakov's works. Once again the discussion was simultaneously being conducted at the highest levels, and even among members of the Politburo. Aleksei Rykov, then the Soviet Premier, dropped an informal note to Stalin early in 1928, after the new head of the Repertory Committee, Fyodor Raskol'nikov, had sought to maintain the ban on *Zoyka's Apartment*: 'Koba! [this was Stalin's Party nickname] Yesterday I was at the Vakhtangov Theatre. I remembered that at your suggestion we overturned the Repertory Committee's decision to ban *Zoyka's Apartment*. It turns out that the ban has not been overturned. A. Rykov.'[25] Stalin had seen the play a couple of times, and apparently enjoyed it. Within a day, the Politburo had passed a resolution to lift the ban on the play in view of the fact that it was 'the Vakhtangov Theatre's only means of existence'.[26] *Zoyka's Apartment* was finally banned on 17 March 1929, after 198 performances.

Having two plays to think about during 1926 might have seemed like a large enough challenge for Moscow's newest fashionable playwright, but astonishingly Bulgakov had a third commission under way at the same time. In late January 1926 he had signed a contract with the Kamerny Theatre for a comedy under the title *The Crimson Island*. His confidence by now was at its peak: he may not have known the details of the debates about him among the leaders of the Communist Party, but he would certainly have been aware that somehow or other he had very influential advocates speaking up for him every time his works were threatened with bans. The staging of his plays also brought him considerable wealth by the standards of the day – a net income of nearly 20,000 roubles in 1927, and 11,000 roubles in 1928, at a time when manual and white-collar workers alike might expect to receive approximately 1,000 roubles a year.[27] His works were garnering him critical controversy as well as sold-out houses: Moscow was turning him into a celebrity.

The Crimson Island took some time to complete. The original contract signed on 30 January 1926 required him to deliver the script to the Kamerny Theatre by 15 July, but though he made a good start on it that spring, the necessity of getting *The White Guard/The Days of the Turbins* and *Zoyka's Apartment* into production that autumn compelled him to set the task aside. In the event, he only succeeded in submitting the text in March 1927, too late even for the following season, and after a long delay permission to stage the play was granted by the Repertory Committee in September 1928, possibly after another intercession by the influential writer Maksim Gor'ky.[28] The premiere of this play on 11 December 1928 was greeted by a critical outcry, including an article in *Komsomol'skaya Pravda* (Komsomol Truth) by Ilya Bachelis deploring the prevalence of 'Bulgakovism' in the theatres of Moscow.[29]

The Kamerny Theatre saw *The Crimson Island* as a project to be worked on in the spirit of traditional Russian fairground theatricals, a modern 'bouffonade'. Once again, the drama text was born out of a prose narrative, a short story with the same title that Bulgakov had published in *On the Eve* in April 1924. At that stage the plot involved an ebullient parody of the February and October Revolutions of 1917, with the primitive natives of a tropical island losing their king in a volcanic eruption, enduring the illusion of democracy under a dissembling and opportunist leader called Kiri-Kuki (modelled on Kerensky), who is in cahoots with colonial foreigners (represented by characters from the novels of Jules Verne), and finally liberating themselves in a further uprising to create a truly 'crimson' (that is, Red, Bolshevik) island. This 'red-and-white' account of the two revolutions of 1917 was just as schematic as Mayakovsky's representation of the same events had been in his *Mystery-Bouffe* (1918, 1921), where a biblical flood functions in the same way as Bulgakov's volcanic eruption to symbolize the February 1917 Revolution and the overthrow of Tsarism. In the Kamerny Theatre's dramatic version of *The*

Crimson Island, this story has become the plot of a play written by a fictional playwright, Dymogatsky, who in this respect figures as a kind of pro-Bolshevik artist like Mayakovsky, writing simplistic propaganda. But his play has itself become a play within another play. The outer framework of Bulgakov's new work is a drama about the difficulties a theatre faces in staging Dymogatsky's play: the eccentric director, the histrionic actors and above all the theatre's struggle to obtain permission to stage Dymogatsky's play from the hostile and thoroughly stupid censor, Savva Lukich. Clearly the experiences Bulgakov had already endured with his attempts to stage his two other plays had prompted this meta-theatrical reflection on the current plight of the artist in Soviet Russia, in a theatrical world which he now knew through and through, and which still filled him with exasperation as well as delight.

The play is subtitled 'A dress rehearsal . . .' because the day when Dymogatsky delivers the play (late) to the theatre turns out also to be the last opportunity to get censorship permission for

The Crimson Island (with volcano, and natives of the tropical island fighting a stylized battle).

the following season: so the theatre has to improvise a full dress rehearsal for the censor even before the cast has had time to read the play through. Savva Lukich, the censor, was recognizably made up and costumed to look like that enemy of Bulgakov and the Moscow Art Theatre, Vladimir Blyum, who had made it his business over the years to campaign against all satirical drama that could be construed as criticism of the Soviet state. In October 1927 Blyum published a piece denouncing the Moscow Art Theatre for staging *The Days of the Turbins* for a second season, and complained that this was no way for the theatre to mark the sacred tenth anniversary of the October 1917 Revolution. He entitled his article 'The Beginning of the End of the Moscow Art Theatre', an infuriating gibe. Bulgakov's retaliation was witty and ingenious, with deadly serious undertones. Savva Lukich attends the last part of the play, and is obsequiously ushered on to the stage, ironically taking up his position on the mock-up of a ship owned by the capitalists, and then settling himself on the throne of the former tyrannical monarch of the island. Despite the evident pleasure he takes in all his own play-acting, he decrees that the play cannot be permitted because its message is insufficiently pro-Bolshevik. The playwright Dymogatsky (by now sounding much more like Bulgakov than Mayakovsky) protests against Savva Lukich with a cry for creative freedom: 'A malevolent old man simply turns up . . . and with one stroke, one flourish of his pen, he ends my life . . . Here, here's my breast, just pierce it with your pen . . .'[30] This represents one of the earliest appearances of the figure of the downtrodden, harried writer in Bulgakov's works. And he could have had little idea just how prophetic these words were about to become, within just a year's time. In the text a hasty new, 'more ideologically correct' ending is improvised, with the ship's parrot calling upon the proletarians of the world to unite and the Western sailors joining in the international revolution, and the play is finally allowed to be staged. *The Crimson*

Island itself was staged 62 times at the Kamerny Theatre between December 1928 and June 1929, before being banned for good.

Bulgakov's life in the mid-1920s could only be described as a success story. In August 1927 his newfound wealth had allowed him to move with Lyuba into a comfortable five-room apartment in the southwestern district of central Moscow, not far from the beautiful Novo-Devichy Monastery. Inside the apartment, two steps led to a small landing in front of a carved oak door with a bronze handle in the shape of a bird's claw: this was his book-lined study, with the large desk at which he always wrote, one leg curled up beneath him, often at night, and with candles burning as well as a lamp. There was a maid, Marusya, who stayed with them for several years, a cat and kittens and, eventually, a dog.[31] Bulgakov would make up comical messages to Lyuba, supposedly written by the animals – and all of them appeared together in the amusing booklet called

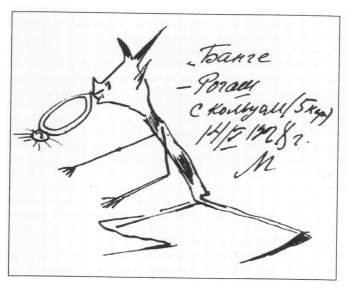

Cartoon by Bulgakov from 14 January 1928, in which Rogash offers Banga a five-carat ring. 'Banga' was one of Bulgakov's nicknames for Lyuba.

Bulgakov's writing desk, later 1920s.

The Torment of Maka (*Muka Maki*), written and illustrated by their close friend Natalya Ushakova. Here at last he had recreated the material comfort and civilized surroundings of his childhood home in Kiev, the goal he had aspired to since he first arrived in Moscow in 1921. But at the same time, Bulgakov's successes were increasingly under threat. His scrapbook of hostile reviews grew and grew:

The cartoon book *The Torment of Maka*, depicting Lyuba's delight when the new kitten, 'Sellout', chases away the rats.

and gradually M[ikhail] A[fanasyevich]'s attitude of stoicism towards them was worn away, and at the same time his nervous system began to suffer: he became more irritable and more suspicious, he began to have problems sleeping, and he developed a nervous tic, twitching his shoulder and his head.[32]

However, none of this deterred him from embarking on the writing of yet another new play, once again in collaboration with the Moscow Art Theatre. This seemed appropriate, since the historical subject-matter of *Flight* followed on naturally from that of *The White Guard/The Days of the Turbins* in the sense that it focused on the plight of the White movement one year further on, in 1919–20, rather than in 1918–19. The protagonists come from a similar social background to the Turbins. The action of the new play is not set in Kiev, but instead describes the Whites as they are driven by the Bolsheviks out of Russia through the Crimea and into emigration, across the Black Sea to Constantinople, and then to Paris. In some respects, therefore, *Flight* serves as the continuation of the novel

The White Guard, which had originally been planned as the first part of a trilogy of novels. The first version of the play was written between 1926 and 1928, although Bulgakov would return to the text and make significant alterations to it during the 1930s, when his hopes were briefly raised that the play might be staged. Most of the work on the first draft was accomplished during the spring and summer of 1927, while *The Days of the Turbins* and *Zoyka's Apartment* were still the talk of Moscow. In April Bulgakov had signed a contract with the Art Theatre, in which he undertook to deliver the text by 20 August. He drew particularly on two sources for his inspiration for *Flight*. Firstly, he insisted that Lyuba recount in detail her own experiences of Constantinople and Paris. Her 'innocent' perspective did much to shape the character of Serafima in the play, the well-born young woman who is abandoned by her cowardly husband, denounces the White General Khludov for his barbarous cruelty, travels into emigration in a fever, and eventually decides to return to live in Soviet Russia with her devoted lover Golubkov. Bulgakov's second major source was the memoirs of a White General, Yakov Slashchov-Krymsky, the prototype for his General Khludov, who had returned to Soviet Russia from emigration in 1921 despite his crimes during the Civil War, and was allowed to remain alive and to work there. The third main protagonist in the play is the weak but honourable 35-year-old intellectual Golubkov, whose love for Serafima governs all his actions and choices (one of the play's earlier titles was *Serafima's Knight*). Golubkov's name, a near-anagram in Russian of the name 'Bulgakov', as well as his age (Bulgakov's at the time of writing), identify him as another of Bulgakov's semi-autobiographical fictional characters.

Although the phrase 'flight of fancy' does not really have an exact counterpart in Russian, this is effectively what the play *Flight* involves: a journey Bulgakov undertook in his imagination in 1927, wondering what it would have been like to go into emigration, as he had so nearly done from Batum on the Black Sea in 1921.

Bulgakov's alter ego in the play, Golubkov, has no strong political convictions, and the nostalgic pull of Russia is enough to persuade him to return home. The author seems to conclude, as he did in *The White Guard*, that running away is always futile, and that you should stay with your native land and share in whatever comes next. The title of *Flight* in Russian (*Beg*) denotes not only the flight of the Whites away from the advancing Bolsheviks and out of Russia, but it suggests the idea of life running its course, and above all the image of a race. But here the races are debased, in a motif that simultaneously demonstrates the complete ignominy of the lives of the Whites in Constantinople and evokes the pointlessness of life as a fugitive. The formerly heroic General Charnota squanders all the money he possesses on the cockroach races run in Constantinople by the sinister Artur Arturovich, the 'Cockroach Tsar'. Meanwhile, General Khludov suffers recurrent dreams about cockroaches scurrying off a kitchen table, only to fall into a bucket.

When he came back to the Moscow Art Theatre with this play, Bulgakov set the director and the backstage staff some extraordinary challenges, pushing them to go beyond the famous skills they had developed in staging realist drama, and to create a production that would border on the surreal. In an extraordinary formal innovation, he couched the eight successive episodes of this play not as conventional scenes but as 'dreams'. This suggests the presence of an overarching consciousness, a narrative perspective such as drama normally lacks. Many productions of the play therefore choose to have the character Golubkov read out all the lengthy stage directions, which are full of lyrical and psychological details. Each new 'dream' requires its own extremely elaborate set, and involves very complex lighting and sound effects, as well as spectacular moments such as the station window, which shatters at the sound of heavy artillery to reveal a line of lampposts from which hang corpses draped in sacks. In this bold play we see Bulgakov's creative imagination at work when he was at the height of his powers. The mind of the author seems to 'dream' the journey into exile, and concludes that it can only lead to nightmares. This seems – for however brief a time – to sum up how Bulgakov felt in 1927–8 about the question of whether he should have gone into emigration or not. His confidence in his decision may have been somewhat shaken, however, when he put in an application on 21 February 1928 to travel abroad to Berlin and Paris, requesting two months to go and sort out his financial affairs with regard to a certain Zakhar Kagansky, who had been pocketing his royalties abroad. The authorities refused to grant him a passport for foreign travel, without providing any explanation.[33]

Bulgakov continued to work on his draft of *Flight* in 1927–8, and by April 1928 the Art Theatre was making plans to stage it during the 1928–9 season. However, on 9 May 1928 a meeting of the Repertory Committee concluded that the play was unacceptable, on the grounds that it showed the tragedy of the honourable Whites in a sympathetic light, while the few Bolshevik protagonists to feature in the work were vulgar and violent. All summer long there were meetings and discussions of possible alterations to the text between the theatre, the Repertory Committee and Bulgakov, but the person whose influence really made a difference was once again the writer Maksim Gor'ky, recently returned to the USSR after having spent seven years living abroad, largely for his health. His warm support for the work and conviction that it would be a great success apparently won the day. Bulgakov's work also had supporters among the political elite: one senior cultural mandarin, Aleksei Svidersky, was emboldened to point out that it would have been completely unconvincing if Golubkov and Serafima, who long to return to Russia to see the snow and the streets of St Petersburg, had instead been made to claim that they were burning to participate in the industrialization of the USSR. The liberal Svidersky went on to say: 'If the play has artistic merits, then we, as Marxists, should consider it to be a Soviet play. And in fact we should abandon terms such as "Soviet" and "anti-Soviet".'[34]

On 11 October *Pravda* announced that the play had been permitted, and the following day Bulgakov signed a further contract for it to be staged in Leningrad as well. But the triumph was short-lived. Gor'ky left the USSR again, to return to the milder climate of Italy for his health (he suffered from tuberculosis). Bulgakov's opponents on the Repertory Committee campaigned relentlessly in the press and at meetings for the decision to be overturned. Ilya Bachelis described Bulgakov's ideas as 'the philosophy of a disappointed cockroach' (II, 736). An OGPU report dated 25 October 1928 commented on reactions to this controversy in Leningrad:

> Soviet . . . people regard him as a figure hostile to Soviet power, who exploits legal opportunities to the maximum in order to battle against Soviet ideology. Those who are hostile or critically disposed to Soviet power literally 'worship' Bulgakov as someone who, while being a clearly anti-Soviet writer, succeeds in propagandizing his own ideas with skill and subtlety . . . In literary and theatrical circles they do nothing but talk about this play.[35]

A further OGPU report on 10 November revealed how closely he was being spied upon now, since individual comments by him on his supporters and his opponents were quoted almost verbatim.[36]

The matter was then referred to the Politburo. Early in January 1929 each member of that body received a full account of the play (it ran to 3–4,000 words), drafted by the *Izvestiya* critic Richard Pikel. He concluded that the staging of *Flight* would represent 'A step backwards for our entire policy on theatre, and it would serve to create a gulf between one of our strongest theatres and the working-class spectator.'[37] In the middle of all these debates, the tension of the situation was exacerbated by the startling news that on 11 January 1929 General Slashchov-Krymsky, Khludov's prototype, had been murdered, apparently by a relative of one of his Civil War victims. The Politburo's final recommendation about the play at the end of January was simply that it would be inappropriate to stage it at the present time.

However, a playwright called Vladimir Bill'-Belotserkovsky drafted a letter on behalf of a number of Communist writers, in which he protested to Stalin about *Flight*. On 2 February 1929 Stalin sent him a lengthy response, containing a remarkably detailed glimpse of his views about Soviet theatre, and revealing him to be something of a liberal in his opinions at that moment, rather than a hardliner. Once the contents became known, however, and perhaps despite its author's actual intentions, the consequences for Bulgakov were disastrous. Rather like Svidersky, Stalin began by arguing that it was not appropriate to apply Party political criteria to works of literature:

> I consider the very premise of the question about the 'right' and the 'left' in fiction (and therefore in theatre) to be incorrect. The notion of 'right' and 'left' in our country at present is a Party matter, specific to the inner workings of the Party. People of the 'right' or 'left' are those who diverge in one or another direction from the pure Party line. And for this reason it would be strange to apply these concepts to such a non-Party sphere, and one which is incomparably broader, such as fiction, and theatre etc. . . . With regard to fiction it would be more accurate to operate with concepts such as 'class', or with the concepts 'Soviet', 'anti-Soviet', 'Revolutionary' or 'anti-Revolutionary'.

Stalin then turned to the specific subject of Bulgakov's play and, like his predecessor Tsar Nicholas I, offered some suggestions as to how the text of *Flight* could be improved:

> *Flight* is the manifestation of an attempt to evoke pity, if not sympathy, towards certain strata in the anti-Soviet world of the emigration – that is to say, an attempt to justify or

semi-justify the White cause. In its present form *Flight* represents an anti-Soviet phenomenon. All the same, I would have nothing against the staging of *Flight* if Bulgakov were to add one or two dreams to his eight dreams, where he would depict the inner social wellsprings of the Civil War in the USSR, so that the spectator should understand . . . that the Bolsheviks, in driving out all these 'honourable' supporters of exploitation, were carrying out the will of the workers and peasants, and for that reason were acting completely correctly.

Finally, Stalin considers the reasons for the success and popularity of Bulgakov's plays, and especially of *The Days of the Turbins*:

Why are the plays of Bulgakov so often staged? It must be because there is a lack of *our* plays that are suitable for the stage . . . As for *The Days of the Turbins* in particular, then it is not that bad, for it does more good than harm . . . If even such people as the Turbins are obliged to lay down their arms and submit to the will of the people, admitting that their cause is utterly lost, then that means that the Bolsheviks are invincible . . . *The Days of the Turbins* offers a demonstration of the all-conquering power of Bolshevism.[38]

One might add that there is a strange paradox about Stalin's reading here of Bulgakov's two plays. It is just about possible to imagine an interpretation of *The Days of the Turbins* that, while admitting its sympathy for White ideals, nevertheless esteems the work for its unexpected value in showing the audience how mighty the opponents defeated by Bolshevism had been. This is presumably how Stalin justified to himself his frequent attendance at performances. But if we look closely at *Flight*, then surely its message is one of utter disillusionment with the White cause. General Khludov is haunted by the ghost of the White orderly Krapilin, executed after accusing Khludov of cruelty. The General turns to suicide (or in other versions of the play, returns to the USSR to face his judges) because he comes to recognize the justice of those accusations. Khludov has in any case become entirely disenchanted with the White leaders, scorning the incompetence and the cowardice of the White Commander-in-Chief (a thinly disguised General Wrangel'), and openly contemptuous of the equally cowardly and hypocritical church leader Archbishop Afrikan. *Flight*, in fact, was neither 'pro-White' nor 'anti-Soviet'.

Be that as it may, and notwithstanding the fact that Stalin's letter had evidently been intended to moderate the hostility of attacks against Bulgakov, his choice of a word such as 'anti-Soviet' with regard to *Flight* meant that once the content of this letter became widely known, the Moscow Art Theatre felt it had no alternative but to abandon all thought of staging the play. Bulgakov felt this rejection of his favourite play as a terrible blow, and as a betrayal by the overcautious theatre.

Quite apart from wrecking the chances of *Flight*, a passing reference Stalin made in the same letter to Bulgakov's *Crimson Island* as 'pulp literature', and to the Kamerny Theatre as 'truly bourgeois', led to the run of that play being terminated in June 1929.[39] *The Days of the Turbins* and *Zoyka's Apartment* were both taken off as well, and by the summer of 1929 all Bulgakov's theatrical triumphs of the previous three years lay in tatters. This had not perhaps been Stalin's overall intention, but these developments reflected a battle that was beginning to be fought in the Party hierarchy over Soviet culture, and Bulgakov became one of its most conspicuous victims. Between 1926 and 1929 he had benefited from a relatively tolerant attitude within the Party, promulgated in a decree on literature published in *Pravda* on 1 July 1925, in which the issue of 'fellow-travellers' had been addressed. This term in Russian means exactly the opposite of what it does in English. Far from describing Westerners with Communist sympathies, in Russian the term was applied during the 1920s to writers of bourgeois origin who had no sympathy for Communist ideology, but nevertheless were not fighting against it, and who were prepared to work within the Soviet state. The 1925 decree recommended tolerance towards them for the time being, partly because of their possible usefulness in training up a new generation of working-class writers, but also in the hope of converting some of them to Communist beliefs in the longer term. At the same time, the Party was aware of the iconoclastic extremism and arrogant intolerance of some groups of hard-line proletarian writers and critics, and there were those who were keen to rein them in: many of the Party leaders in fact had rather traditional tastes in literature and art. During the NEP era the Party rejected the notion of creating a monolithic literary organization in favour of allowing free competition between different groups and tendencies. This approach was rapidly losing favour in the second half of the 1920s as Stalin began to sideline his rivals within the Party, both on the right and on the left, and to consolidate his absolute authority. The Party followed the fierce press debates about culture very attentively, and as we have seen, often devoted full Politburo sessions to discussing and deciding the fate of a given work and its author. Bulgakov's ruin in 1929 may have come about almost despite the will of several highly placed figures in the Party, including Stalin himself, but cultural policy in general was about to become very much more rigid and oppressive.

Bulgakov must have had some inkling of the debates about himself, of course, and clearly hoped that his advocates could still rescue the situation. He therefore resolved to appeal for help to the highest authorities in the land, using the simple expedient of sending them some letters describing his plight. He had already shown himself unafraid to raise his grievances with highly placed individuals: in 1926 he had sent letters to the OGPU, to Aleksei Rykov (who had succeeded Lenin as Chairman of the Council of People's Commissars in 1924), and later on to the man responsible for cultural affairs, Anatoly Lunacharsky, demanding the return of *The Heart of a Dog* and of the diaries that had been confiscated. In the summer of 1928 he wrote again to the OGPU, to Genrikh Yagoda in person (who in the 1930s would become notorious as one of those who implemented Stalin's Terror), referring to Gor'ky's recent promise to intervene in the matter.[40]

He resorted to this strategy again in July 1929, when he drafted the first of his several letters to Stalin and other highly placed Party members, which on this occasion was addressed also to Maksim Gor'ky. These documents are striking for their tone, formal in parts and familiar in others, but clearly written in the expectation that his indignation would be taken seriously. Describing how he had written four plays in the previous four years, all of which were now in jeopardy, he also recalled the hostile reviews his works had received, his treatment at the hands of the OGPU in 1926, and the many prose works of his which had been banned. In addition, he tells of how he had been refused permission to travel abroad, concluding:

Bulgakov's brother Nikolay (Kolya) in Paris, 1920s.

Bulgakov's brother Ivan (Vanya) in Paris, 1930s.

At the end of ten years my strength is broken. Since I am no longer capable of surviving, since I am persecuted, and since I know that I cannot be published or staged any more within the confines of the USSR, and since I have been reduced to nervous exhaustion, I am turning to you and requesting your intercession before the Government of the USSR TO EXILE ME BEYOND THE BORDERS OF THE USSR TOGETHER WITH MY WIFE L. YE. BULGAKOVA, who joins me in this request.

This letter was forwarded to the Politburo for consideration with sympathetic notes from Svidersky and others, but for some reason – perhaps because Stalin was away at the time – the question was shelved at a meeting in early September. Further letters sent to a member of the Central Committee, and to Maksim Gor'ky, seem to have had no effect and received no reply (VIII, 252–66). During that summer, Bulgakov poured his heart out to his brother Nikolai, who was now working as a medical scientist in Paris, and who did all he could to help his brother with handling his foreign publications. Having described to him all his reverses, Bulgakov concluded:

> If my request is turned down, then I can consider that the game is over, it's time to put away the cards and blow out the candles . . . Without being fainthearted, I can tell you, dear brother, that the question of my demise is just a matter of time, unless of course, a miracle comes to pass. But miracles rarely happen.[41]

However, his apparently hopeless situation would be relieved some months later, but not so much through a miracle as because of a tragedy – the shocking and unexpected death of Vladimir Mayakovsky in April 1930.

4

'The Years of Catastrophe', 1929–36

Although Bulgakov would describe 1929, with the banning of all four of his plays by early summer, as his 'year of catastrophe',[1] there were nevertheless other things going on that betokened new beginnings. In February he made the acquaintance at a dinner party of a married woman called Yelena Sergeevna Shilovskaya (1893–1970). An exceptionally attractive dark-haired woman, just a little younger than himself, she had long been aware of Bulgakov as a writer:

> Somehow he stood out as someone unusual, with unusual themes, and his language, his point-of-view and humour were unusual . . . I was the wife of Lieutenant-General Shilovsky, who was a fine and extremely honourable man. We had what you could call a happy family: a husband who occupied a distinguished position, two lovely boys . . . And altogether everything was fine. But when I chanced to meet Bulgakov, I understood that here was my fate, despite everything, despite the insanely painful tragedy of breaking up the family.[2]

With her husband away on a trip, Yelena started to spend every day with Bulgakov, going skiing or to the opera, or else to the actors' club, where he and his literary rival Mayakovsky played billiards, and Mayakovsky said ruefully that he could scarcely keep the cue in his hands, such was the passionate intensity of Yelena's gaze, willing Bulgakov to win. On one occasion Bulgakov woke her in the middle

Yelena Shilovskaya, 1928.

of the night, took her at 3 am to a square called Patriarchs' Ponds, pointed to a bench and declared mysteriously: 'this is where they first saw him.' Then they went on to visit a strange apartment nearby, where two men (whose names she never discovered) entertained them to a feast of caviar and wine by an open fire, and the older man, charmed by her kiss, declared her to be a witch.[3] Readers familiar with Bulgakov's *Master and Margarita* will of course recognize moments here from the novel, especially the suddenness and absoluteness of their falling in love with each other, and 1929 marks the beginning of an intensive period of work on the opus that would eventually be considered his masterpiece. Bulgakov, whose marriage with Lyuba had drifted in recent years towards increasing detachment, pursued Yelena with letters, photos and dried flowers when she went away on holiday to the Caucasus that summer. On her return in September he presented her with an exercise book containing the first draft of what in the later 1930s would become his *Theatrical Novel*, although at this point it bore the title *To My Secret Friend*. For the next year and more he and Yelena met whenever they could, and the relationship became increasingly ardent. However, when Shilovsky found out the full truth, he demanded that they cease all contact. As Yelena put it: 'I lost my nerve and decided to stay with my husband, and didn't see Bulgakov for 20 months, having given my word that I would not accept a single letter, would not answer the telephone, nor go out alone on the street.'[4] Losing this new love would plunge Bulgakov into deep misery from early in 1931 until the summer of 1932.

But in the meantime his newfound personal happiness and feeling of exuberance renewed his creative energies, and between October and December 1929, notwithstanding the banning of his earlier plays, he embarked on a new and entirely unexpected project. All four of his earlier plays had engaged with contemporary Russian life, or the recent past. *The White Guard/Days of the Turbins*, together with *Flight*, had represented his attempts to write historical plays about Kiev, the Crimea and emigration, covering the years from 1918 to 1920. In *Zoyka's Apartment* he had turned his attention to life in Moscow under NEP. And then in *Crimson Island* he had not only conjured up the events of the Revolution and Civil War years (1917–21), but he had set them inside a framework in which he raised issues of censorship relevant to the later 1920s. Each of these endeavours to comment on topical issues had run into difficulties in the increasingly fraught ideological atmosphere of Soviet Russia, and all of them had now come to naught. In these circumstances, Bulgakov decided that this would be a good moment to apply his overflowing theatrical imagination and talents to an entirely different project, one that might take him into less controversial territory. He decided to write a historical play about the life of the playwright Molière, a subject apparently far removed in time and place from the problems of life in Soviet Russia.

> I have read and re-read Molière and loved him since I was a child. He had a great influence on my formation as a writer. I was drawn to the personality of this teacher of many gener-ations of dramatists – a comedian on stage, but an unsuccessful, melancholic and tragic man in his personal life.[5]

Using for the most part pre-Revolutionary accounts of Molière in Russian, together with some French sources, Bulgakov created a work that focuses mostly on Molière's private life and on his role as artistic director of his theatre. He shows him falling for the young actress Armande, a relationship that, according to gossip, might in fact have been, unbeknownst to him, incestuous. Bulgakov also shows him successfully negotiating his relationship with Louis XIV, but then falling out of favour when the Church, outraged at his satirical depiction of a hypocritical priest in *Tartuffe*, succeeds in turning the great monarch against him. When we first see Molière on stage, he flatters the Sun King by saying he believes he will become famous for the very fact of having performed during Louis XIV's reign. But Bulgakov chose for the epigraph to his play the eighteenth-century inscription adorning Molière's bust in the Académie Française: 'Rien ne manque à sa gloire. Il manquait à la notre' (His glory lacks nothing; it is he who was lacking for ours). This suggests the opposite, the powerful conviction which Bulgakov held that art would endure instead, and would outweigh the ephemerality of political rule. The play's title, *The Cabal of Hypocrites*, derives from the historical 'Cabale des dévots', which functioned under the auspices of a Catholic secret society, the Compagnie du Saint-Sacrement, and was notorious specifically for its attacks on Molière's *Tartuffe*. One interesting feature of Bulgakov's depiction of the period is the way in which he paints the cabal, Archbishop Charron and the Catholic Church as the truly sinister and evil forces which mass against Molière and even apply pressure to the king to achieve their goals. The autocratic Louis XIV, by contrast, is depicted as a shrewd judge of character who is not unsympathetic to the artist. When critics attacked this play, one of their concerns was the possibility of controversial analogies being drawn between the operations of the Church and the Communist Party, with Stalin emerging, like the Sun King, as someone whose hands were sometimes tied by circumstances. Certainly, if Bulgakov had any inkling of the differences in opinion between Stalin and other Party officials over his play *Flight*, and any hopes that Stalin might sway opinion in his favour, then we can understand the relatively positive picture of the ruler painted in his Molière play.

By the time Bulgakov wrote this play he had worked with several different Moscow companies and directors, and had gained a bold sense of all the possibilities that sets, design and other technical dimensions of theatre could achieve. As in *Flight* and *The Crimson Island*, he set exciting production challenges for the theatre with every successive scene. The opening scene of the play places the audience backstage at the Palais-Royal Theatre, looking from the dressing rooms up to the stage, where a further curtain will eventually be drawn to reveal a glimpse of the auditorium beyond. This device fosters in us an acute awareness of the extent to which the dramatic action is 'staged', and each successive scene only reinforces this: Molière hires an illusionist whose harpsichord seems to be able to play itself (in reality the young Moirron is hidden inside, and will go on to deceive his new master in other ways as well). In the second act, life at court is presented as an entirely staged affair, with the Sun King's card-playing, his use of a jester to 'punish' a cheat, his dining and his going to bed all choreographed and scripted performances designed to intimidate onlookers. In Act III, the secret meeting of the Cabale des dévots is an elaborate ritual attended by masked men and enacted in a darkened crypt; the following scene, with Archbishop Charron portrayed as a demonic figure in the confessional as he extorts the story of possible incest from Molière's former mistress, Madeleine, is shaped by extravagant use of organ music and the singing of a choir. A particularly effective moment closes Act III, as the archbishop squabbles with the aristocrat he had hoped would murder Molière in a duel, and they resort to spitting at one another, only to be interrupted by a haughty Louis XIV, who apologises for disturbing them. The final act returns us to the Palais-Royal, where the actors debate whether to go ahead and complete a performance of *Le Malade imaginaire* in view of the violence threatened by the audience, and it is agreed that the show must continue. Molière then collapses and dies on stage, surrounded by grotesquely masked doctors. This is an entirely apt (if historically inaccurate) end for a man whose entire life has been theatre, and who rises to his true greatness only on the stage. Like Shakespeare before him, and Chekhov after him, Molière was a playwright who lived and worked with the theatre company that staged his plays. Bulgakov was on his way to becoming an in-house dramatist in a similar way at the Moscow Art Theatre.

In another of those dramatic innovations that bring Bulgakov's plays so close to his prose writing, he once again, as in *Flight*, introduced a kind of external narrative perspective on the course of events for the audience's benefit. Here it is the actor Lagrange, who takes no part in the Act I performance for the king. Instead, he sits quiet and still, a figure of some mystery and authority, with a prince-like demeanour. His role is to chronicle the events of company life in his 'Registre', to which he adds coded signs to indicate great moments (a lily to mark the presence of the Sun King) or tragic ones (a large black cross to denote the death of Molière). His quality of omniscience provides a perspective within the dramatic tale that seems to belong to the seventeenth century, while also being shared with posterity. His presence serves to suggest to us that the essential truth about the past can be known, even if Bulgakov's biographical project strays occasionally from the literal facts. As he said himself: 'I wrote a Romantic drama, not a historical chronicle. In Romantic drama full biographical accuracy is neither possible nor necessary.'[6]

That autumn Bulgakov would also begin to take on the role of a chronicler with regard to himself. Convinced, on the one hand, of his own talent, and aware, on the other, of how difficult it was becoming for him to be published or staged, he took a decision to create a personal archive. He preserved all the drafts of his works, and started keeping copies of the letters he wrote to friends as well as those he received, so that posterity (and grateful literary scholars) would be able to reconstruct his literary life in the future, even if it was to be suppressed in the present. In the closing lines of the Molière play, Lagrange had concluded that the cause of all Molière's troubles was in fact fate. And Bulgakov, with this play that he had imagined might restore his fortunes in the world of Soviet theatre, found himself similarly thwarted once again by fate. When he read the new work to the Moscow Art Theatre on 19 January 1930, it was received with delight; but on 18 March the implacable Repertory

Committee placed a ban even on this work set in seventeenth-century France.

There had been plenty of signs over the previous months that proletarian groups (and in particular the Russian Association of Proletarian Writers, or RAPP) had seized a dominant position in literary life. Since the summer of 1929 they had been conducting a vitriolic campaign in the Communist press against other 'fellow-traveller' writers such as Boris Pil'nyak and Bulgakov's close friend, Yevgeny Zamyatin, and they had forced the closing down of some relatively liberal writers' groups which had emerged under NEP. Their goal of silencing a large number of writers was being pursued with no apparent restraining hand from the government. Realizing that, with the ban of the Molière play, his situation had become truly desperate, on 28 March 1930 Bulgakov composed one further, very lengthy letter appealing for an alleviation of his plight. He submitted it on 2 April to Yagoda at OGPU for forwarding to the Soviet government – and on this occasion Stalin did respond.

Describing how some of his friends had been advising him, after the banning of all five of his plays, to write something 'Communist' and recant his beliefs, he commented:

> I did not follow this advice. I would scarcely succeed in appearing in a favourable light before the Government of the USSR if I wrote a letter full of lies, representing a clumsy and indeed naïve political volte-face. I didn't even make an attempt to compose a Communist play, since I knew for certain that I was incapable of writing such a play.

He had collected 301 printed reviews of his work in his scrapbooks, of which 298 had been hostile – and he even quoted some of the more vulgar ones, in which Aleksei Turbin was called a son of a bitch, and he himself was described as someone who picked scraps out of piles of vomit. He went on to argue that the Soviet press was therefore clearly correct when it claimed that there could be no place for him or his writings in the USSR. He also acknowledged that in *The Crimson Island* he had mounted an attack on the dark and malevolent force of the Chief Repertory Committee:

> They are the ones who cultivate helots, toadies and eulogists. They are the ones who are destroying creative thought. They are strangling Soviet drama, and they will succeed in killing it off. I did not express these thoughts in a whisper, in a corner. I included them in a dramatic pamphlet, and I staged that pamphlet in the theatre . . . To struggle against censorship, of whatever kind and whatever the government in power, is my duty as a writer, as are calls for freedom of the press. I am a passionate supporter of that freedom, and I consider that if any writer should think of trying to persuade me that he did not need it, then he would be like a fish declaring in public that it did not need water.

Bulgakov admitted that he personally favoured the processes of evolution over those of revolution, adding that he would continue to depict the Russian intelligentsia as the most worthy class in the nation. He went on to claim for himself with pride the title of satirist, just as he had done during his 1926 OGPU interrogation. The recent ban of the Molière play had represented for him not just the destruction of past works, but had prompted him to cease work on future ones as well: 'And personally, with my own hands, I threw into the stove the draft of a novel about the devil, the draft of a comedy, and the beginning of a second novel, about the theatre.' In conclusion, he appealed to the Soviet government to act humanely and allow him to leave the country with his wife Lyuba. Failing that, he asked them to arrange for him to be taken on as an assistant director at the Moscow Art Theatre – or to be given walk-on parts there, or else employment as a stagehand, 'because at the present moment I, who am well-known in the USSR and abroad as the author of five plays, am facing destitution, the street, and death'.[7]

This heartfelt stream of self-righteousness and indignation was something he had composed with the help of Yelena, with whom he had presumably discussed the delicate decision to ask for permission to take Lyuba with him, if he was allowed to leave the country, rather than Yelena herself. Its relatively informal language and occasionally melodramatic tones might have been expected to create a poor impression on its readers, but it so happened that external events combined to ensure that his plea was listened to. The almost unbalanced intonations of the writing suggested how deeply distressed he really was. The government soon had cause to be concerned about this, because Vladimir Mayakovsky, whose political allegiances had been so much more pro-Soviet than Bulgakov's, shocked the entire nation when he committed suicide by shooting himself just two weeks later, on 14 April. The risk of a second major literary figure following suit would have been very damaging. Mayakovsky's funeral took place on 17 April 1930, and Bulgakov was present at the ceremony when his coffin was removed from the Writers' Club where he had been lying in state. On the very next day Bulgakov received an astonishing phone call.

That evening he rushed round to tell Yelena how Lyuba had picked up the telephone while he was taking a nap, and been told that there was a call for him from the Party's Central Committee. His first reaction was that someone was playing a trick on him, but when he picked up the receiver he was told that Stalin was going to speak to him. Then Stalin's voice, with its strongly Georgian accent, came on the line:

'We have received your letter, and we and the comrades have read it. You will receive a positive reply to it . . . But maybe it's true that you are really asking to go abroad? So, are you really that fed up with us?'

Bulgakov was utterly thrown by all this, and hesitated before replying:

> 'I have been thinking about that a great deal recently – whether a Russian writer can live outside his homeland. And it seems to me that it would be impossible.'
>
> 'You're right. I think that as well. So where do you want to work? At the Moscow Arts Theatre?'
>
> 'Yes, I do. But I have spoken to them about that, and they turned me down.'
>
> 'Well, you send in an application to them. I have a feeling that they will agree. We ought to meet and have a conversation.'
>
> 'Yes, yes! Iosif Vissaryonovich, I very much need to speak to you.'
>
> 'Yes, we need to find a time to meet, definitely. And now I wish you all the best.'[8]

The details of this telephone conversation, noted down afterwards by Yelena from Bulgakov's account of it, may not of course be quite exact. But it was an earth-shattering event that marked Bulgakov for the rest of his life, and certain essential points about it would stay with him forever. Firstly, the very fact that Stalin had decided to speak to him in person over the telephone was testimony to the fact that he was after all considered a truly important figure in the literary world of his day. Secondly, the split-second choice that Bulgakov had to make – whether to insist on going abroad, or to stay in Russia – placed him in an impossible dilemma. If he had said he did want to leave, would he have provoked Stalin's anger? And the question about whether he could flourish as a writer abroad, and indeed how he would feel if he abandoned his relationship with Yelena, clearly represented genuine concerns. His reward on this occasion for committing himself to staying in Russia was to be promised a job in the Moscow Art Theatre. But Stalin also dangled in front of him the prospect of further conversations, and Bulgakov believed him. For the rest of his life he was tormented by this hope, trying to understand why it never came to pass. This use of a personal telephone call was a tactic that Stalin would use occasionally with other writers, most notoriously in the instance of Boris Pasternak and the conversation he had with him in 1934 about the recently arrested poet Osip Mandel'shtam. It persuaded certain individuals, even as the Terror was unleashed, that it might still be possible to speak openly to Stalin himself, that things could be sorted out in a frank conversation between intelligent men. In reality, of course, all this was simply a cat-and-mouse game between Stalin and the intellectuals, which served only to increase Stalin's sense of his own importance.

Bulgakov was now expecting his situation to change, but it took a while for anything to happen, and so he followed up the telephone conversation with a further short letter to Stalin dated 5 May 1930, asking to be received by him in person, since he claimed still to have no means for survival. He did not receive a reply, but on 10 May he was taken on at the Moscow Art Theatre as an assistant director.[9] Bulgakov wrote to Konstantin Stanislavsky on 6 August:

> After my deep sadness about my plays which had perished,
> I felt easier when, after a long pause and now in a new capacity,
> I crossed the threshold of the theatre which you have created for
> the nation's glory. Konstantin Sergeevich, please receive your
> new assistant director with a happy heart. Believe me, he loves
> your Arts Theatre.

Stanislavsky responded in similar tones: 'You cannot imagine how glad I am that you have joined our theatre! With all my heart I welcome you, I sincerely believe in your future success, and would like to start working with you as soon as possible.'[10] However, in a letter written the day after the one to Stanislavsky, Bulgakov complained to his brother Nikolay that in financial terms this post did not do much at first to alleviate his difficulties, since the Art Theatre promptly deducted from his monthly salary of 150 roubles the money he still 'owed' them against his advances after the cancellation of his plays.[11] But at roughly the same time, he was also offered a further job at 300 roubles a month, as an adviser to a theatre known as TRAM (the Theatre for Young Workers), where he stayed until March 1931. These two posts between them guaranteed him financial security in the medium term.

The honeymoon with the Moscow Art Theatre was short-lived. The first task they gave him was to assist with a new stage adaptation of Nikolai Gogol's 1842 novel *Dead Souls*, and by late October 1930 he presented them with a script he had worked on with his usual inventiveness. Since Gogol' had written much of his novel about Russian provincial life while living in Rome, Bulgakov transferred the framework of the action to Italy. And true to his habit of introducing subjective viewpoints in texts where they might not be expected, he created the new role of a 'reader' or authorial persona:

> This is not someone who simply conveys the lyrical digressions to the spectator or presents the action of the show; instead, he is someone who has to communicate and elucidate for the audience the tragic gulf between the Gogol' who was seeking to create a positive hero, and the Gogol' who belonged to that same real world which he felt obliged to mock and show in such devastating satirical colours.[12]

But his version was met by Nemirovich-Danchenko with utter dismay, and when Stanislavsky became involved in February 1931, he was equally critical about Bulgakov's attempts to move beyond a realistic depiction of Gogol's world towards the grotesque. The arguments and repeated disagreements between Bulgakov and the

Art Theatre about his concept for this adaptation would drag on for two years, before the first performances of *Dead Souls* finally took place in November 1932.

On 30 May 1931 Bulgakov, obviously still under the illusion that he could continue a dialogue with Stalin, addressed a further letter to him. He prefaced it with a four-paragraph epigraph from Gogol' in which his predecessor, writing an 'Author's Confession' some ninety years earlier, both justifies his role as a satirist and explains why he needs to travel abroad in order to appreciate Russia properly and write *Dead Souls*. This was an attempt at a 'literary' opening to the conversation, a way of inviting Stalin to engage with him on the level of culture and aesthetics rather than political considerations. This time Bulgakov asked for permission to travel abroad from July until October that year, to revive his creative powers and stimulate them with fresh impressions. Describing himself as a lone, hunted wolf on the literary scene, he explained how his complete exhaustion had led to nervous illness (he had started to suffer panic attacks when left alone, and also when he went out on the street), and for this reason he asked for Lyuba to be given permission to accompany him:

> But as I conclude this letter, I would like to say to you, Iosif Vissaryonovich, that my dream as a writer would consist in being summoned to you in person. Please believe me, that this is not because I would see this as the most advantageous opportunity for me, but also because your conversation with me over the telephone in April 1930 left an indelible mark in my memory. You said to me: 'perhaps you really do need to go abroad . . .'[13]

But absolutely no response came to this plea either, and in August 1931 Bulgakov wrote to his friend Vikenty Veresaev about his despairing mood:

I am suffering from a tormenting misery. And that is
that my conversation with the General Secretary [of the
Communist Party: Stalin] did not take place. For me this is
a horror, the darkness of the grave. I yearn, frenziedly, to
see other countries, if only for a short period. I rise in the
mornings with this thought, and go to sleep with it.[14]

His unhappiness had been compounded that year by the loss of
his relationship with Yelena, after the scandalous scene between
Shilovsky and Bulgakov in late February 1931, and Yelena's guilty
capitulation to her husband's demand that all contact should cease
between them. As well as his professional difficulties, Bulgakov was
now suffering from a deep sense of loneliness.

That summer he wrote a new play for a Leningrad theatre, in
which the Communist state comes under attack from capitalist
forces in a future war, and the city of Leningrad is virtually destroyed
before a new socialist world government comes into being. In this
uncharacteristic work entitled *Adam and Eve*, the only truly convincing and engaging theme is the love story of the heroine, who rejects
a self-assured Communist in favour of an older man, a timid, self-
effacing inventor with no clear political convictions, who longs only
to be left in peace. When this play too was rejected both by the
Leningrad theatre and by the Vakhtangov in Moscow, Bulgakov
seemed neither surprised nor upset.[15]

His renewed state of misery was unexpectedly relieved in the
autumn of 1931, when Maksim Gor'ky once more returned for
a brief visit to the USSR from Italy. During his visit he took the
opportunity to write a glowing review of Bulgakov's Molière play:

The author has achieved a great deal, which only confirms once
again the widely held view of his talent and of his skill as a dramatist . . . I am absolutely confident that the play will be a great success
at the Arts Theatre in Moscow . . . It is an outstanding play.[16]

To Stalin, with whom he maintained a detailed and regular correspondence from Sorrento about literary figures and their works, Gor'ky wrote on 12 November to explain his support as follows:

> Bulgakov is not someone I feel close to, and I have not the slightest desire to defend him. But he is a talented writer, and there are not so many of those in our country. There is no sense in turning them into 'martyrs for their ideas'. An enemy has to be either eliminated, or re-educated. In this particular situation, I'm in favour of re-educating him.

Gor'ky recommended that Stalin should try to see Bulgakov in person, and concluded his letter with his own sentiments about the leader:

> Last summer in Moscow I declared to you my feelings of deep comradely sympathy and respect for you. Allow me to repeat this. These are not compliments, but a sincere desire to tell a comrade: I sincerely respect you, you are a good man and a strong Bolshevik. One's need to express this is not often satisfied. You know this. And I know how hard things are for you sometimes. I shake your hand firmly, dear Iosif Vissaryonovich.[17]

Gor'ky's influence over Stalin – at least for another few years – was almost unparalleled, and he spent many a quiet hour smoking and chatting together with him in the garden out at the *dacha*. Nevertheless, Gor'ky still felt obliged to articulate his deference in this extraordinarily obsequious manner when addressing the Party leader in writing.

Bulgakov was altogether astonished by what seemed an incomprehensible reversal of his previous situation: as a result

Iosif Stalin and Maksim Gor'ky, 1931.

of Gor'ky's advocacy, contracts were suddenly signed in mid-October 1931 for the Molière play to be staged after all, both by the Moscow Art Theatre and the Great Drama Theatre in Leningrad. On 26 October 1931 Bulgakov wrote to two of his closest friends, both of whom were in Leningrad, to tell them the good news.

One of the people he wrote to that day was the writer Yevgeny Zamyatin, who had become a close friend during the 1920s. There was much to draw them together, both in terms of their family

backgrounds and their views about Soviet literature and culture
and the importance of freedom of speech. Zamyatin had written
an anti-utopian science-fiction novel in 1920 called *We*, which had
been banned in the USSR as an anti-Soviet work. However, it had
been published in translation abroad during the 1920s, and it was
these foreign publications that had brought down upon Zamyatin's
head the wrath of the proletarian RAPP group from 1929 onwards.
Like Bulgakov, Zamyatin had effectively been silenced by the end of
the 1920s, and like Bulgakov, Zamyatin took advantage of Gor'ky's
visit to the USSR in 1931 to address via this influential figure a
letter to Stalin and the Soviet government, requesting permission
to leave the country. Whether it was Zamyatin's 'Revolutionary'
past (he had briefly been a member of the Bolshevik party at the
time of the 1905 Revolution), or whether it was Gor'ky's gratitude
towards him for the work they had done together in setting up
new literary institutions during 1917–21, is hard to say, but where
Bulgakov's letter that summer went unanswered, Zamyatin's had
achieved its aims. At the time when Bulgakov informed him of the
licensing of the Molière play for performance, his friend was just
two to three weeks away from leaving the Soviet Union. By early
1932 Zamyatin had travelled as far as France, where he lived until
his death in 1937. He and Bulgakov maintained an intermittent
correspondence during those years, and his success in escaping
must have offered Bulgakov a deeply enviable example of the fact
that leaving the country was still possible – but only for some.

The other close friend Bulgakov wrote to with the good news
about Molière that October was Pavel Popov. As a lifelong practising
Christian, Popov was inevitably going to run into difficulties in the
militantly atheistic USSR, and his academic interest in philosophy
had proved equally controversial, so that in recent years he had
turned to the apparently safer sphere of literary scholarship. He had
a special interest in the manuscripts of Pushkin, and was also one
of a team working on the new ninety-volume edition of the works

of Lev Tolstoy, a role he had been drawn into through his marriage to Tolstoy's granddaughter, Anna Il'inichna Tolstaya. He was an extremely well-educated man, who had seen something of Europe before the 1917 Revolution, and he had an excellent command of languages, including ancient Greek. In February 1930 Popov had been arrested on suspicion of espionage, and although he was released after two months of detention and interrogation, he was then told that he had to go into internal exile, and live away from all the major cities for a period of three years. This was then commuted to a milder punishment (it is possible that his connection with the distinguished Tolstoy family afforded him some protection), but he had been interrogated again in March 1931. After an episode when his wife tried to have him admitted to a mental asylum because of his increasing paranoia, he was expelled from Moscow in the autumn of 1931 and sent to live in Leningrad. These were, to use the phrase of the poet Anna Akhmatova, 'relatively vegetarian times' compared to the Great Terror that was to follow, and Popov and his wife would be allowed back to Moscow six months later.[18] Certain features of Pavel Popov may have been used to create the character of the Master in *The Master and Margarita*, and he and his wife certainly recognized their Moscow home in the description of the basement apartment where the two lovers meet in the novel. But Popov's principal importance for Bulgakov was as a completely devoted and loyal friend, whose unswerving belief in his talent prompted him to talk about compiling his biography. Over the next few years, Bulgakov began to use his letters to Popov to pour out his most intimate feelings about the events of his life, as a kind of substitute for the diary he was now too fearful to keep.

As part of this plan for his letters to document his life for Popov, he numbered his first missive of 1932 'Letter no. 1'. In fact he took from late January until late February that year to write this, and in it he not only described his insomnia and his sense of loneliness, but the astonishing news that in the wake of permission being granted for the Molière play, he had also received a telephone call on 15 January from the Moscow Art Theatre to tell him that *The Days of the Turbins* was being revived as well. Perhaps feeling that he ought to follow Gor'ky's advice and do something himself to alleviate Bulgakov's plight, Stalin had apparently taken the opportunity one day when he was attending a different show at the Art Theatre to ask why they were not currently performing *The Days of the Turbins*.

They replied in some embarrassment that the play had been banned. 'Nonsense,' he retorted, 'It's a good play, and it should be put on. Put it on again.' And within ten days instructions were given that the show should be revived.[19]

As Bulgakov described it to Popov, the news was almost too much to take in:

It is unpleasant for me to have to admit it, but the announcement crushed me. I felt physically unwell. I was flooded with joy, but then immediately with melancholy as well. Ah, my heart, my heart! . . . For reasons which I do not know, and which I am not in a position to assess, the Government of the USSR gave the Arts Theatre the wonderful instruction to revive *The Days of the Turbins*. For the author of that play this means that he, the author, has had a part of his life restored to him. And that is all.[20]

The revival of the play was greeted with enormous enthusiasm by Moscow's theatregoers: tickets sold out as soon as they went on sale, and there were twenty or more curtain calls after the first performance on 18 February 1932, although Bulgakov declined (to Stanislavsky's relief) to go out and take a bow himself.

There was no particular wisdom about my decision, it was a very simple one. I don't want any bows, nor any curtain-calls, and in fact I don't want anything at all, except for them to leave me in peace for the love of Christ, so that I can take hot baths and not be racking my brains every day about what I am to do with my dog when the contract for my apartment runs out in June.[21]

His gloomy mood in this letter to Popov of late April is explained by the fact that no sooner had Bulgakov begun to rejoice over the return of the *Turbins* when startling news reached him from Leningrad in the middle of March. The Great Drama Theatre there had suddenly pulled out of the plan to stage his Molière play, even though it had now been officially licensed for performance, work was already under way on the production, and he had even received an advance on the royalties. The devastating blow, which he described as like being stabbed in the back, had come about this time not because of the actions of the Repertory Committee, but simply because of the machinations of an influential 'proletarian' playwright, Vsevolod Vishnevsky. This man had written a newspaper article in November 1931 challenging the theatre to justify its decision to stage Bulgakov's play about Molière's life – which could surely have neither topical nor political relevance – when they could have been staging the works of the great Molière himself. The Leningrad theatre cravenly took fright at this attack, and decided to abandon the plan.[22] And so Bulgakov was left just with the *Turbins* to show for his career as a dramatist, as well as the slender hope that the Molière play would make it to the stage in Moscow. In that same letter to Popov of 24 April 1932, he recalled how his mother had rather hoped that her sons would one day become railway engineers:

I don't know whether my late mother knows that her youngest son has become a solo balalaika player in France, the middle son is a scientist, a bacteriologist in that same France, while the eldest hasn't chosen to become anyone at all. I have a feeling that she does know. And at times, when in my bitter dreams I see the lampshade, the piano keys, *Faust* and her (and in fact this is the third time in recent nights that I've seen her in my dreams. Why is she disturbing me?), I want to say to her: 'Come with me to the Arts Theatre. I'll show you a play. And that is all I can offer. Peace, mama?'[23]

Ten days earlier, still pouring his innermost feelings out to Popov on a night when he had found himself wide awake at 5 am, he had confessed:

Every night now I look not ahead, but back, because I cannot see anything for myself in the future. In the past I have made five fateful mistakes. Had it not been for them . . . I would not be writing, soundlessly moving my lips in bed at dawn, but as one should, sitting at a writing desk. But there is nothing to be done now, you can't bring anything back. I only curse those two attacks of unexpected timidity which assailed me like a swoon, and because of which I committed two out of the five mistakes. I have an excuse: this timidity was a passing thing, the product of my exhaustion. I have an excuse, but that is no consolation.[24]

Biographers of Bulgakov have spent much time trying to work out what these five fateful mistakes might have been, but among them are surely: his failure to emigrate from the Black Sea port of Batum in 1921; his acceptance of General Shilovsky's insistence that Bulgakov's relationship with Yelena had to cease; and his hesitation when Stalin asked him in 1930 if he really wanted to leave the USSR, which might conceivably have allowed him to escape the country.

In the meantime he had begun to undertake a number of lesser tasks to fill his time and try to keep afloat financially: one of these was an adaptation for the stage in the autumn of 1931 of Tolstoy's *War and Peace*, intended for that same Great Drama Theatre in

Bulgakov playing the part of the Judge in *The Pickwick Papers* (1933–4).

Leningrad. In 1933–4 he persuaded the Art Theatre to let him do some acting, and played the part of the Judge in a production of *The Pickwick Papers*, astonishing and impressing Stanislavsky with his performing skills. There were also a couple of minor commissions relating to Molière: a 'Molieriana', a light farce in the autumn of

1932 loosely based on Molière's *Le Bourgeois gentilhomme*, followed by a translation of *L'Avare* in the winter of 1935. But he also embarked on a more substantial Molière project, a prose biography of the French dramatist as a contribution to the well-known series 'Lives of Famous People'. This idea, which had come about at Gor'ky's behest, would surely be a safe undertaking, and Bulgakov worked away at it throughout the hot summer of 1932, and on until the spring of 1933. Writing to his brother Nikolai after he had submitted the manuscript on 5 March that year, he commented:

> I can no longer recall for how many years, if you include the beginning of my work on the play, I have been living in the luminous, fairytale Paris of the XVIIth century. And now evidently, I am bidding farewell to it for good. If fate should take you to the corner of rue Richelieu and rue Molière, think of me! Greetings from me to Jean-Baptiste de Molière![25]

But once again, Bulgakov's insistence on introducing a subjective viewpoint to a genre that was expected to be objective caused difficulties. His narrator describes himself as a figure wearing a long coat with large pockets, holding a goose quill rather than a steel pen, and he records an imagined conversation with the midwife who in January 1622 has no inkling of the significance of the premature boy child she has just delivered. She is astonished when he tells her that this child will become even more famous than the kings of France, and that his writings will be translated even in wild Muscovy, that 'cold and terrifying country. There is no enlightenment in that country and it is populated by barbarians who speak in a tongue which would be strange to your ear' (V, 38). The narrator ridicules the many trite books which will be written about Molière and about his death, and argues that their descriptions have nothing to do with the truth about the man he calls his 'poor, bloodied master', using a term which will become famous in Bulgakov's descriptions of other writer-heroes subsequently. Bulgakov concludes his biography wistfully with another glimpse of the statue of Molière above the fountain: 'And I, who am fated never to see him, send him my farewell greetings' (v, 38–41, 246). The series editor Aleksandr Tikhonov was not persuaded, however, by Bulgakov's unconventional project:

> You have placed between Molière and the reader some sort of imaginary storyteller, from whose point of view the narrative is directed. Of itself, as a device this might have been very fruitful, but the problem is that you have not selected the type of narrator entirely successfully. This strange person not only does not know about that rather well-known method in the USSR, the Marxist method of historical researching of historical phenomena, but he is also entirely alien to any kind of sociological approach even in the bourgeois sense of that term. Why does the figure you have drawn of Molière stand entirely apart from the social and historical conditions in which he lived and worked? What was the class structure of France in Molière's time? What class or group did Molière himself represent? Whose interests were served by his theatre, etc.? We need to know all this . . . If, instead of this casual young man in an old-fashioned coat, who from time to time lights or puts out the candles, you had given us a serious Soviet historian, he would have been able to tell us many interesting things about Molière, and about his times.[26]

Tikhonov was also concerned that there were several moments in the biography where fairly transparent allusions were made to the plight of the writer in the modern-day USSR.

In these comments, which predictably led to the plan to publish Bulgakov's Molière biography being shelved, we can see the outlines of the new literary policy which was emerging in these years, and which would dominate the rest of the Soviet era. Stalin had come to agree with Gor'ky that the vindictive squabbles at the end of the 1920s between literary factions, whether proletarian or otherwise, were getting out of hand. Between 1932 and 1934 plans were drawn up to amalgamate all the different literary groups into a single organization which would then come directly under the government's control. This was to be the Soviet Union of Writers, which held its founding Congress in Moscow in the summer of 1934. One of the main purposes of the work of the Congress was to promulgate a new path in literature called 'Socialist Realism', as the official method of both literature and literary criticism in the USSR. The aim of Socialist Realism was the depiction of historical reality in a way that combined a traditional, realistic approach with features which would highlight progressive tendencies in individuals and society, in other words, those aspects of life which most clearly promised to take the country forward towards the 'bright future' of fully realized Communism. Tikhonov's challenging questions about Bulgakov's project were precisely the kind of editorial and critical response that over the next fifty years would attempt to mould literary texts into a single, homogeneous, ideologically charged entity. On this occasion Bulgakov responded quite uncompromisingly, pointing out that he was not a historian but a dramatist:

> And since that is my position, I can affirm that I see my Molière quite individually. My Molière is in fact the only true Molière (from my point of view), and I did not choose the form which would convey that Molière to the audience for no reason, but with great care.

He therefore declined to rewrite it : 'Let's bury it and forget it!'[27] The work was only published for the first time by 'Lives of Remarkable People' in 1962.

This further setback, involving the rejection of yet another of his works, was one that Bulgakov took relatively calmly. Perhaps one of the reasons for this was that in the meantime he had rediscovered the personal happiness which he had thought lost forever, and been reunited with Yelena. She had kept her promise not to see him for twenty months, but as she put it, fate intended otherwise:

> Because the first time I did go out on to the street, I met him, and the first phrase he uttered was: 'I cannot live without you.' And I replied: 'Nor can I without you.' And we decided that we would be together, come what may.[28]

By early September 1932 General Shilovsky wrote to inform Yelena's parents in dignified and courteous tones that his marriage to their daughter had come to its natural end, that he did not reproach her for anything, and that they were parting as friends. His attitude towards Bulgakov himself may not have been quite so restrained. Be that as it may, Shilovsky and Yelena were divorced on 3 October 1932, and she and Bulgakov married the very next day, Bulgakov having sent a conspiratorial note marked 'Secret. Urgent' to one of the Art Theatre's directors, requesting permission to be let out of a meeting early so that he could attend the ceremony.[29] Yelena's older son Yevgeny stayed with his father, while six-year-old Sergei moved in with his mother to Bulgakov's apartment (Bulgakov hastily found Lyuba somewhere to live elsewhere in the same building).[30]

For the first time, Bulgakov had the experience of his own family life, and as he described it in a letter about their lives together to Zamyatin and his wife the following spring, it was something he turned out to enjoy very much: 'We passed the winter by the stove with extremely interesting tales about the North Pole and about hunting elephants, we fired shots from a toy pistol, and we were continuously ill with the flu.'[31] Perhaps having been the eldest in a large and happy family himself partly explains it, but according to Yelena, Bulgakov seems to have been very at ease with both her children, and evidently became a very good stepfather to the younger boy, playing lots of games and taking him on outings, while insisting upon high standards of behaviour.[32] They were all very pleased when it became possible for them to move at last into a new flat in a writers' cooperative in March 1934, with gas for hot water and a bath. 'For M[ikhail] A[fanas'evich] the word "apartment" is a magical word. There is nothing in the world of which he is envious, except of a good apartment!'[33] There was constant irritable anxiety about money and the difficulty of collecting fees – and retaining them after works were, as so often, abandoned. Over a period of several years the Moscow Art Theatre, for example, kept demanding the return of the 3,000-rouble advance he had received for *Flight*, on the grounds that it had been banned. 'Show me the ban!' retorted Yelena, reflecting the infuriating lack of clarity that surrounded all these decisions.[34] But in general the family appears to have been reasonably well off in the early 1930s, with enough money for regular entertaining, a new piano and smart new clothes when required. But above all Bulgakov was extremely happy with his new wife, whom he trusted completely and would come to rely on more and more during the all too short years of their shared lives.

One task with which he entrusted her from 1 September 1933 was keeping a diary, since he had resolved never to do such a thing again himself after the mortifying experience of having his notebooks confiscated by the OGPU in 1926. Yelena's diary is an invaluable document, providing detailed glimpses of their social life, their visitors and of their feelings about all the further setbacks that awaited Bulgakov with his work. It also discreetly reflects the atmosphere of Moscow during the Terror, with brief and laconic comments charting the disgrace, arrests and deaths of numerous friends and acquaintances, as well as weary entries recording the inescapable presence in their flat of a variety of individuals who, as they clearly suspected, were present in order to report on the writer's words to the authorities.

Bulgakov and Yelena in April 1935.

In the spring of 1934, and again in 1935, Bulgakov put in applications for them to travel abroad to France or Germany. This was his perennial theme: 'I am a prisoner . . . I have been artificially blinded . . .'.[35] But Yelena's unsympathetic sister Ol'ga was sceptical:

> What would prompt them to give Maka a passport? They give them to those writers who will be sure to write a book that is useful for the USSR. But has Maka shown in any way since Stalin's telephone call that he has altered his views?[36]

In May 1934 they were told that there would be a favourable outcome, and they even saw their two passports on a table, waiting for them. Afterwards, he wondered whether it was some incautious joking that he and Yelena indulged in as they completed their last forms in that office; or perhaps the question of their permission to travel was still in fact in the balance; but the actual handing over of the passports was postponed. A day or two passed, and then they waited longer and longer until they were finally told after a few weeks of agonized uncertainty that they could not travel after all. This was at a time when other writers of their acquaintance, not to mention other members of the Art Theatre, were being allowed abroad. Bulgakov wrote a detailed complaint to Stalin about the injustice of this rejection, pleading with him to intercede and pointing out that any suspicion that they would stay abroad if allowed to travel there could scarcely be justified, given that it would mean parting Yelena from her children.[37] But once again he received no reply. All of this took a tremendous toll on Bulgakov's health, and he became terribly anxious, fearing death, and so agitated that he could not go out anywhere on his own. Yelena accompanied him to and from all his meetings, and took over the management of his business affairs and contracts as well. In the end he turned to a hypnotist for help, and was very pleased with the success of his treatment. Yelena recorded with relief the first evening when he managed to go out on his own in half a year, in late November 1934.

Bulgakov had good reason to become fearful that spring. The poet Osip Mandel'shtam was arrested on the night of 13 May and taken away from his apartment in the same building on Nashchokinsky Lane where Bulgakov was now living. Mandel'shtam was initially sent into internal exile in the northern Urals, where he attempted suicide before being granted permission with his wife Nadezhda to live in a city closer to Moscow. Nadezhda recorded his words to her: 'What are you complaining about, it's only in our country that they respect poetry enough to kill people for it.'[38] Mandel'shtam eventually died in a labour camp in 1938. The poet Anna Akhmatova visited on several occasions at this time from Leningrad, not just to hear Bulgakov reading parts of *The Master and Margarita*, but to take advice from him about how best to approach Stalin and appeal for mercy when first of all Mandel'shtam and then in October 1935 her own son and husband were arrested.

The silencing of writers and banning of their works was moving into a new phase, when their very physical survival was at stake. Yelena also noted an occasion in late November 1934 when Stalin came to see *The Days of the Turbins* together with the Leningrad Party leader Sergei Kirov, who was murdered, quite possibly at Stalin's instigation, just three days later. This event is generally held to have unleashed the main thrust of the Terror.

Bulgakov's next major literary undertaking was another biographical play about a writer, this time taking as his subject Russia's national poet, Aleksandr Pushkin (1799–1837). There was a certain amount of calculation in this decision, as the centenary of Pushkin's death was coming up in 1937, and it was a fairly safe bet that in the increasingly patriotic mood of the country during the 1930s the centenary celebrations would be a massive event. Theatres would be falling over themselves to stage plays about Pushkin, so his decision to embark on the project during the summer of 1934 reflected some careful forward planning. After the setbacks he had been experiencing – and with the ongoing nightmare constituted at this time by the endlessly protracted rehearsals for the Molière play at the Art Theatre – Bulgakov decided on a further strategy to safeguard the outcome for this new play. Soon after he had sketched out a plan for the work, he took it to Vikenty Veresaev, who was a much-respected scholar over twenty years older than himself. In the mid-1920s Veresaev had assembled a documentary chronicle of Pushkin's life using the memoirs and letters of his contemporaries, which provided an unparalleled resource for biographical studies. Bulgakov was also drawn to Veresaev because of the similarities in their professional lives: Veresaev had, like himself, started out in life with a medical career, and had written a volume called *Notes of a Doctor* in 1900 which had been a great literary success, and provided a worthy precursor to Bulgakov's own *Notes of a Young Doctor*. Bulgakov had got to know Veresaev shortly after his arrival in Moscow, and their friendship had developed to the extent that Veresaev had lent him money at a particularly difficult moment. In December 1934 the two men signed a contract agreeing to work together on the project, with Veresaev supplying the historical materials while Bulgakov drafted the play itself.

Given that the occasion for staging this play was to be the centenary of Pushkin's death, Bulgakov decided to make the focus of his project the final weeks of Pushkin's life. Indeed the play, which he always simply referred to as *Aleksandr Pushkin*, came to be known after his own death as *The Last Days (Pushkin)*. This was a story that was known to every Russian: the great poet, still only in his thirties, was married to the young and beautiful Natal'ya, who apparently took little interest in his work and instead enjoyed the frivolous pleasures offered by life at Court. It was whispered that Tsar Nicholas I himself found her very attractive, and he awarded Pushkin a humiliatingly low rank at Court in order to oblige the couple to stay in St Petersburg, when what the poet longed for was to retreat to his country estate where he wrote his best poetry. Natal'ya had also attracted the attentions of a French cavalry officer, Georges d'Anthès, who was in St Petersburg under the protection of his adoptive father, the Dutch envoy van Heeckeren. It was said that d'Anthès had married one of Natal'ya's sisters only in order to be closer to the real object of his affections. After a series of very public scandals, Pushkin fought a duel with d'Anthès in which he was fatally injured, dying just a few days later.

Just as in his Molière play, Bulgakov's principal focus here was on the several forces that combined during the reign of an authoritarian monarch to harry the brilliant writer towards an early grave. Precisely one of the points of contention he was struggling over with Stanislavsky at the time was the issue of how Molière should be depicted on the stage, with Stanislavsky wanting him to be shown, quill in hand, composing works of genius, while Bulgakov was determined to avoid all such clichés. When it came to writing the biography of a national hero like Pushkin, Bulgakov was even more anxious to avoid anything trite of this kind. The radical expedient he resorted to in this play, therefore, was simply to create a work depicting the final weeks of Pushkin's life in which the poet himself never appears, except as a figure fleetingly glimpsed passing across a doorway at the back of the stage. As Yelena reported it, he would have considered it vulgar to give Pushkin physical embodiment: 'It seemed to him unthinkable that an actor, however talented, should come out on stage in a curly wig and sideburns, and give a peal of Pushkinian laughter.'[39] Instead, Bulgakov showed the strained atmosphere in his household, the malicious gossip of his literary rivals, the flirtation between Nicholas I and Natal'ya, the witnesses to the duel, and finally the outpouring of popular grief and student outrage at the news of Pushkin's death, while the authorities bury him in haste to avoid any further demonstrations. This is a play in which the action on stage is constantly extended by a sense of other things going on just out of sight, in unseen rooms of Pushkin's apartment, down below the bridge where van Heeckeren anxiously watches the duel, through windows where characters can see events that the audience cannot, or simply outside in the street as the snowstorm which provides one of the play's leitmotifs intensifies. Bulgakov compensates for Pushkin's absence as 'a writer of genius' through the creation of one of the few non-historical characters in the work, the police spy, Bitkov. He is a simple man who comes and goes in the apartment disguised as a clock repairman, and spies on Pushkin's every word without apparently comprehending the significance of what he is doing. In this play it is he who unwittingly plays the part of the objective, omniscient chronicler of events. But he is also spellbound by the poetry he has to learn in order to report it back to the authorities. At the end of the play he begins to realize that something untoward has been going on, since he has been deliberately sent elsewhere on the day of the duel so that there should be no risk of it failing to go ahead. He is a representative of the common Russian man, and he is one of the few who, like Pushkin's friend and fellow-poet Zhukovsky and Natal'ya's sister Aleksandra, show their genuine appreciation of the haunting beauty of Pushkin's poetry by singing or reciting it. The play is framed by phrases from one of Pushkin's most famous poems drawing on folk themes, *Winter Evening*, in which the poet sits dreamily with his aged nanny while a snowstorm howls outside.

Bulgakov had signed a contract for the Pushkin play with the Vakhtangov Theatre in December 1934, and on 2 June 1935 he held a reading for them where he and Veresaev as co-authors shared the applause, even though their relations would sour over the following months. During 1935 Veresaev became more and more dissatisfied with Bulgakov's concept, and after some heated disagreements in which he reproached Bulgakov for disregarding the historical truth, Veresaev withdrew his name as co-author of the work, although it was agreed that he would nevertheless continue to be entitled to 50 per cent of the royalties. At this stage the Moscow Art Theatre also became interested in the new work, and a further reading was arranged for their actors and directors at the end of August. The Repertory Committee gave permission for the play to be staged on 20 September, and after that the two theatres began to wrangle about who should stage it. Other theatres within Russia also approached Bulgakov about putting it on, and there were discussions with Sergei Prokofiev about turning it into an opera. Dmitry Shostakovich and the distinguished conductor Aleksandr Melik-Pashaev also read the text. Rehearsals got under way, and for once everything seemed to guarantee future success for a work whose interpretation was uncontroversially admiring of the great poet, even if the way of approaching the subject was somewhat unusual. With sickening inevitability, however, the catastrophe that was to befall the Molière play in March 1936 dragged the Pushkin play down with it, and this became yet another of Bulgakov's works that failed to reach the stage.[40]

The story of the Moscow Art Theatre's work on the Molière play had turned into a long-drawn-out nightmare during the early 1930s, and over the four years of rehearsals even the actors themselves had come to detest the project. After the initial signing of the contract on 15 October 1931, in which the theatre undertook to stage the work not later than 1 May 1933, the whole thing got bogged down in the perennial rivalries between the theatre's two founders, Stanislavsky and Nemirovich-Danchenko. Rehearsals took place sporadically, and Bulgakov, who was present in his official capacity as assistant director, became more and more morose. On 14 March 1935 he wrote to Popov about his complete exasperation:

Stanislavsky has now taken charge. They ran through *Molière* for him (without the final scene, which wasn't ready), and he, instead of discussing the production and the acting, started to discuss the play. In the presence of the actors (in the fifth year of rehearsals!) he started telling me that Molière was a genius, and how this genius should be described in the play. The actors greedily rejoiced, and started asking for their parts to be expanded. I was seized by fury. I was intoxicated with the desire to chuck the notebook at them and say – you go ahead and write about geniuses and non-geniuses, but don't try to teach me, I won't be able to do it in any case. It would be better if I did the acting instead of you. But you can't, you can't say that! I repressed all that, and began to defend myself. Three days later, the same thing again! He stroked my hand, and said that I needed to be stroked, and then off he went in the same way. To cut a long story short, I have to write something in about Molière's significance for the theatre, and somehow demonstrate that Molière was a genius and so on and so forth. All of this is primitive, pathetic, and unnecessary! And now I'm sitting with my copy of the text, and my hand refuses to lift itself.[41]

Bulgakov was also infuriated by the endless acting exercises Stanislavsky made the actors do as part of his 'Method', training them to use a cane properly or wear a feathered hat stylishly, rather than focusing on finalizing the performance.[42] The authorities were also beginning to become concerned about the state of affairs in the theatre, and eventually the production was handed over towards the end of 1935 to Nemirovich-Danchenko, who unexpectedly seized the opportunity to praise Bulgakov in the theatre's in-house journal:

> Bulgakov is just about our brightest exponent of dramatic technique. His talent for developing an intrigue, for keeping the audience in a state of tension throughout the whole show,

Konstantin Stanislavsky in the mid-1930s.

Bulgakov at the dress rehearsal of *Molière*, 5 February 1936.

for drawing images and developing them, and for leading the spectators towards a certain keen notion is absolutely exceptional.[43]

In February and March 1936 the play was finally deemed ready for dress rehearsals and previews. Despite its hugely enthusiastic reception by the audiences, the first reviews in the Party-controlled press were largely hostile, criticizing the work for reducing the figure of the great French opponent of religion, hypocrisy and social injustice to a weak and indecisive individual. The issue was taken up in a lengthy memorandum addressed to Stalin and to the state premier Vyacheslav Molotov on 29 February 1936 by Platon Kerzhentsev, then chairman of the State Committee for the Arts. Kerzhentsev quoted dialogue from the play which he felt demonstrated that

M. Bolduman (Louis xiv) in the Moscow Art Theatre production of Bulgakov's *Molière*.

Bulgakov, despite the skill with which he had fashioned the play, was making blatant allusions to the position of writers under the dictatorship of the proletariat. The theatre, he said, had spent excessive amounts on the lavish set and costumes, to produce what was in effect a typical bourgeois drama. Kerzhentsev's recommendation was that the play should not be banned outright, but that the theatre should be prompted to realize that it had deviated from the precepts of Socialist Realism, and 'make its own decision' to take the play off. The best way to achieve this would be to place a sharply worded editorial in *Pravda*, criticizing the play along these lines. Stalin's response was to pen an instruction as follows: 'To Molotov.

V. Stanitsyn (Molière) in the Moscow Art Theatre production of Bulgakov's *The Last Days* (1936).

In my opinion Comrade Kerzhentsev is right. I am in favour of his proposal. I[osif] Stalin.'[44]

This was a tactic that had already been used to shattering effect a few weeks previously, when a notorious *Pravda* editorial of 28 January 1936 under the title 'Cacophony instead of Music' had denounced Shostakovich's opera *Lady Macbeth of Mtsensk* (there would be a further such editorial on 6 February attacking his ballet music). On 9 March the unsigned editorial attacking Bulgakov's Molière play was published under the title 'Superficial Glitter and False Content'. As soon as Bulgakov saw the article he declared that that was the end of the play (and of another light-hearted comedy

Bulgakov (wearing his 'Master's' cap) and Yelena, 1936.

of his also then in rehearsal, *Ivan Vasil'evich*). Sure enough, when he and Yelena went to the Art Theatre later that same day the play had already been taken off, after fewer than ten performances. On 16 March Bulgakov was summoned to a meeting with Kerzhentsev, who criticized both the Molière and the Pushkin plays, and he realized that the latter was doomed as well. Over the next few months there were a couple of half-hearted attempts to re-open the question of these two productions, but in the increasingly nervous atmosphere of the Terror they came to nothing. In mid-September Bulgakov resigned from his job at the Moscow Art Theatre, which had helped to sustain him since Stalin's telephone call in 1930. As he told Veresaev: 'I have left the Arts Theatre. It was painful for me to work in the place where *Molière* perished . . . Peace to the ashes of Pushkin, and peace to us. I will not disturb him, let him not disturb me either.'[45] He would never really forgive the Art Theatre for the haste with which they had rushed to abandon the Molière play. On 5 October 1936, Bulgakov wrote to Popov with bitter irony:

Give orders for a bottle of Veuve Clicquot to be brought up from your cellar, and drink to the health of *The Days of the Turbins*, for today the play marks its tenth anniversary. I am doffing my greasy writer's cap to my old woman, my wife congratulates me, and that's the entire celebration.[46]

5

The Master and Margarita, 1936–40

If 1929 had been for Bulgakov his first 'year of catastrophes', 1936 was proving to be the second, as once again all his plays which had been in the course of production were swept from the stage and declared to be ideologically unacceptable. The last seven years had included moments of deep misery, especially when he was parted from Yelena, but there had been moments of joy and of hopefulness as well. And during those same years, even though his life had become such a public spectacle and he was being closely watched and reported on by official stooges, Bulgakov nevertheless succeeded in carrying out a further huge and vital project in complete secret, hidden from the prying eyes of the authorities – the writing of his great novel, *The Master and Margarita*.

In his letter to Stalin of March 1930, he had mentioned that alongside the first chapters of a novel about the theatre (which later in the 1930s would become his unfinished *Theatrical Novel*), he had also consigned to the stove the beginning of 'a novel about the devil'. This project appears to have begun to take shape in his mind during the second half of 1928, and he told Popov early in 1929 that whereas the image of his mother had provided the starting point for his novel *The White Guard*, this time it was the image of his father, Afanasy Bulgakov, that had inspired him. His father's scholarly investigations into Western approaches to Christianity offered a model of respectful interest in the subject of religion, which was completely at odds with the crass militant atheism promoted by Bolshevik ideology. In his diary for 5 January 1925, Bulgakov had recorded his feelings of outrage after a horrified visit to the brand-new 'Godless' publishing house, whose publications painted Jesus Christ as a swindler and scoundrel (VIII, 106). He might have moved away personally from the religious faith and practice of his childhood, but this kind of philistine assault on the cultural values of European civilization was something he found intolerable. So the initial stimulus for the new novel was a reflection on attitudes to the Christian faith in the USSR.

In line with his new scheme to create a literary archive for himself and for posterity, Bulgakov did not destroy his first draft in its entirety, but preserved the spines of his notebooks, so that some fragments of text have survived. Further notebooks dating from 1929 to 1931 have also been preserved. One of the possible titles for the work at this stage seems to have been 'The Black Sorcerer'. The second major theme of the novel makes its appearance after the disasters of his career in 1929, when Bulgakov extends his satire of contemporary Moscow society to the self-serving worlds of modern literature and of the theatre. He then set aside the drafts until after his separation from Yelena had been brought to an end with the happiness of their marriage in the autumn of 1932, at which point he swiftly completed seven chapters, some of them dictated to her and therefore preserved in her handwriting. But when Bulgakov heard on 12 October 1933 that his playwright friend Nikolay Erdman had been arrested, says Yelena, he frowned; that night he burned a further portion of his secret novel.[1] As he continued work on the text during the summers of 1933 and 1934, in breaks from his work for the Art Theatre, the third major theme of the work emerged, the deep love between the persecuted writer and his courageous and devoted mistress. Nevertheless, the novel would not acquire its definitive title of *The Master and Margarita* for some years to come, not until 1937 or 1938. During the mid-1930s he would give readings of certain chapters of the novel at home, to a very limited circle of his closest friends, but the number of people who were even aware of the text's existence during his lifetime was tiny. He revisited the text from time to time, and the novel would undergo several further revisions until the summer of 1938. At that point he undertook a complete review of it and had the entire novel typed up by Yelena's sister Ol'ga, who worked at the Art Theatre as Nemirovich-Danchenko's personal assistant, and who smiled, according to Bulgakov, just once in the course of the entire dictation. As he wrote to Yelena, who was away on holiday:

> And what will come of it, you ask? I don't know. Probably you will put it away in a desk, or in the cupboard where my murdered plays already lie, and occasionally you will remember it . . . I have already come to my own conclusion about this thing, and if I can just improve the ending, I will consider that the thing is worth revising, in order for it to be put away into the darkness of a drawer . . . From your distance you cannot see what this final sunset novel has done to your husband after his dreadful life in literature.[2]

During 1939 and 1940 he returned to the text when he could, even during his final illness, and he made his last corrections to the work approximately one month before his death. But an entire quarter of a century would then pass before *The Master and Margarita* created a sensation, even with its first, heavily cut, appearance in print during the Thaw period, in two separate issues of the journal *Moskva* (Moscow) late in 1966 and early in 1967. It was first published in full in the Soviet Union in 1973.

In this extraordinarily inventive and complex novel, which is so unlike anything that came before it in Russian literature, one fundamental preoccupation binds the various levels of the narrative together: *The Master and Margarita* is above all things a vindication of the subjective vision of the artist. When the mysterious figure of Woland (who later turns out to be the Devil) first makes his appearance in Moscow, he chooses to interrupt a conversation between two literary men. The magazine editor Berlioz is explaining to his younger colleague, Ivan Bezdomny, that his recent poem about Jesus Christ will not pass muster with the authorities, because in portraying Jesus as a wicked man he has implicitly suggested that he did exist, whereas of course the correct line would be to deny that he had ever existed at all. Woland's mission to Moscow is essentially to investigate Russian society in the age of atheism, and to consider what has happened to personal morality under the new dispensation. His conclusion, of course, is that despite the best propaganda efforts of the Bolsheviks, human nature has not changed, and that people behave much as they ever did, succumbing to temptations just as they always have. Woland and his retinue, alternately comical and terrifying, wreak havoc as they mete out reprimands to the inhabitants of Moscow, and they apparently condemn Berlioz to be run over by a tram as a particularly savage punishment for his unbelief. Their performance of magic tricks at the Variety Theatre ends up exposing all the petty vices and peccadillos of the audience members, so that the stage here becomes the forum for the revealing of truth.

Another purpose of Woland's visit to Moscow is to hold his annual spring ball there, and for this, according to tradition, he needs to find a woman named Margarita to host the occasion with him. The encounter between Margarita and Woland comes about, therefore, initially by chance. But when she is offered a reward for her services, she demands the return of her beloved Master, a writer who has been arrested, ending up in a lunatic asylum because of a book he has written. The Master had burned his book in despair after it was rejected for publication by Berlioz and his like, but Woland magically restores it to him with a comment that would go on to become one of the most famous phrases from the novel: 'Manuscripts don't burn.' This affirmation of the enduring power of art to survive political contingency and adversity had of course acquired increasing urgency in the atmosphere of the Terror.

Four chapters of Bulgakov's *Master and Margarita* are constituted by the Master's text, which offers the reader a kind of fifth Gospel. The encounter between Christ and Pilate, together with the Crucifixion, are narrated in a way that is at once wholly recognizable, and yet entirely different from the familiar texts of the Bible. Bulgakov did extensive research into the historical accounts of the period and recent studies of the subject (Ernest Renan, Frederic W. Farrar, David F. Strauss), and provides a narrative that is wholly convincing in its historical detail. The figure of Christ – who appears here under the Hebrew or Aramaic name of Iyeshua – is stripped of any supernatural powers, although he is nevertheless an original thinker and a man of peace with healing gifts who completely fascinates Pilate. This narrative becomes centred on a sympathetic portrayal of Pilate, and the guilt he feels for allowing Iyeshua to be killed.

One of the features of the novel's structure which can make it seem so complex, particularly on a first reading, is that the four chapters about Christ and Pilate are clearly part of a single text – they are written in a style that is quite distinct from the rest of the novel, and they also form part of a continuous narrative, even if they are interrupted by other sections of Bulgakov's novel. When we read (together with Margarita) the last of these chapters set in Yershalaim (Bulgakov's rendering of the name Jerusalem), it becomes quite obvious that all these four sections belong in the Master's novel. Yet the earlier chapters had been offered to us first as a story told by Woland to Berlioz and Ivan, and next as dreams that Ivan has when he too has taken refuge in the lunatic asylum where the Master lives. This seemingly contradictory device, presenting entirely different sources for what is one single narrative, serves to suggest that what the Master has done is to record a vision, a higher truth about what really happened some

2,000 years earlier. That truth is naturally available to Woland, who belongs to the realm of the beyond; and it is granted to Ivan in a dream to reward him as he turns away, in the course of *The Master and Margarita*, from disbelief towards belief in the existence of the Devil and of Christ. The Master himself will eventually come to understand the supreme significance of what he has written, exclaiming: 'Oh, how I guessed it! Oh, how I guessed it all!' (VI, 245)

Bulgakov's decision to offer his readers a brand-new version of the Christian story is clearly not for doctrinal reasons as such. The novel suggests that his version is historically accurate, but Bulgakov does not provide this in order to enter into a polemic with other competing interpretations of the story of Christ. We may recall here his father's openness to different ways of approaching the Christian faith, from the Western as well as the Eastern Church. But in a world such as that of the USSR, where churches have been closed, priests executed and religious instruction all but banned, Bulgakov seems to have felt that there was an urgent need for people to renew their awareness of one of the fundamental narratives of Christian culture. The Yershalaim chapters of *The Master and Margarita* perfectly fulfil the function of *ostranenie* ('defamiliarization/making strange'), first identified by critics of the Russian Formalist school in 1919. Where something has become so familiar that it risks becoming a cliché, it loses its power to move us. The creative artist therefore has to find new ways to present the familiar, so as to startle us into refreshing our perceptions. When reading the Yershalaim chapters, we are constantly disconcerted when minor details clash with our preconceived expectations of the Gospel narrative. The overall effect of this is to clear the way for a story in which we are invited to evaluate afresh the character of Pontius Pilate. He is presented as a lonely man whose closest companion is his dog; he suffers from excruciating migraines, and is tormented by his failure to protect Iyeshua and by his longing to meet him again in order to continue their absorbing conversation.

In certain respects, he reminds us of General Khludov from *Flight*, who also yearned to forget the sins and weak moments of his past.

Bulgakov's novel provides no explanation as to why and how the Master has been granted this unique vision of the historical truth about the past; it is not something he has deserved because of any particular deed or virtue. He attempts to offer his narrative for publication in Moscow, but the critics of 'Massolit', the writers' organization which very closely resembles the Soviet Union of Writers, turn the work down and start a campaign of persecution against him. They are depicted eating lavish meals at the restaurant for the Writers' Club, Griboedov House, while the true artist is reduced to penury and acute nervous strain. Only the courage and loyalty of Margarita can rescue him from his plight, and her service as a witch at Satan's ball earns her the restoration of her lover and of his manuscript. But the text has a further surprise in store for the Master. He and Margarita are released from their lives in the here-and-now to travel towards a new destiny in the afterlife. On the way, they are brought to where Pilate sits, tormented by his desire to be reunited with Iyeshua. The Master is now empowered to become an active agent within the story he himself has written down, and he frees Pilate to walk up a moonbeam to rejoin Iyeshua, thus bringing to a close the purgatory that Pilate has suffered for two millennia. After this, the Master is permitted to settle with Margarita in a quiet Romantic home, with windows wreathed in vines and music to listen to. He has not been a heroic figure, but he has pursued his artistic vision to its full conclusion. He is therefore awarded a destiny that echoes what Aleksandr Pushkin yearned for in his later years, and surely reflects Bulgakov's most heartfelt wish during the 1930s, as he entered his fifth decade. In *The Master and Margarita* the final judgement passed on the Master is that 'he has not earned the light, he has earned peace' (VI, 504).

Alongside the tensions of Moscow life as the Terror got under way, these years had also seen an extraordinary episode in Bulgakov's life that offered a complete contrast to the daily grind. This improbable glimpse of an altogether different life within the confines of Moscow was offered by the staff of the American Embassy, who arrived there towards the end of 1933, when the decision was made in Washington that diplomatic relations with the USSR should at last be established, in view of the need to form alliances in the face of the increasing threat from Japan. The first U.S. ambassador, William Bullitt, visited the Moscow Art Theatre in December 1933 and was hugely impressed by *The Days of the Turbins*, which he ended up seeing at least five times, having requested a copy of the text directly from its author in April 1934. Once he had been introduced to Bulgakov, he began to extend invitations to him and to Yelena to attend film shows and à la fourchette suppers at his official residence, where they found themselves meeting the ambassadors of France, Romania and Turkey, as well as the French writer Antoine de Saint-Exupéry, who told them tales of his flying exploits and showed them card tricks. The Bulgakovs were also befriended by some of the ambassador's more junior staff, including the exuberant interpreter Charles Thayer, as well as Charles Bohlen and George Kennan, both future ambassadors to the USSR themselves. Kennan at the time wanted advice from Bulgakov about the life of Chekhov he was working on. These contacts with the Americans led to proposals that Bulgakov's works be translated for the American theatre, as well as encounters with the visiting cast members of a Yale University group which had staged the *Turbins*. The Americans came round to the Bulgakovs' apartment for suppers of caviar, salmon, pâté, radishes, cucumbers, baked mushrooms, vodka and white wine.[3] The foreign visitors were always accompanied by a certain Zhukhovitsky who, as Yelena records, was someone who attached himself to Bulgakov and was constantly pressing him to come out with explicit statements about his attitude to Bolshevism and the Revolution. Other 'friends' at this time similarly urged him to try writing a play about a factory, or about the re-education of criminals in labour camps, such as the notorious construction site for the White Sea Canal where many prisoners perished.

In April 1935 the Bulgakovs received an invitation card to a ball at the ambassador's residence, an occasion that had been consciously planned to be the social event of the decade, an opportunity to show the Russians just how spectacular and lavish American hospitality could be. Charles Thayer was charged with organizing the occasion together with Irena Wiley, wife of the embassy counsellor, and he regaled the Bulgakovs afterwards with some of the complicated and hilarious situations he had had to deal with in making all the arrangements. Yelena left a full account of the event in her diary:

> M[ikhail] A[fanas'evich] was in a dark suit, and I was wearing an evening gown in blackish blue with pale pink flowers. We arrived there towards midnight. Everyone was in tails, there were just a few dinner-jackets and ordinary jackets . . . Bohlen and Faymonville came down to greet us in the vestibule, and to assist us. Bullitt charged Mrs Wiley with the task of entertaining us. In the hall with columns people were dancing, and there were multicoloured projectors from the galleries. A mass of birds were fluttering about behind a net. There was an orchestra which had been brought in from Stockholm. M[ikhail] A[fanas'evich] was most of all enchanted by the conductor's tailcoat, which reached down to his heels . . . In the corners of the dining hall were little pens, containing kid goats, lambs, and bear cubs. On the walls there were cages with cockerels. At about three in the morning the accordions started up and the cockerels started to crow. *Style russe* . . . There was a mass of tulips and roses – from Holland. On the upper floor there was a kebab stall. Red roses, and French red wine. Downstairs there was champagne everywhere, and cigarettes. We wanted to leave at about three, but the Americans wouldn't let us go . . . At about six we climbed into an Embassy Cadillac and were

driven home. I brought an enormous bouquet of tulips home, a gift from Bohlen.[4]

Readers of *The Master and Margarita* have been astonished to discover, since the publication of this passage from Yelena's diary, that in a novel where very few episodes can be correlated to actual events in Soviet life, the real-life American Embassy Ball of April 1935 finds reflection quite unmistakably in one of the most fantastic scenes of the novel, the scene of Satan's Ball. The fictional ball, with its black jazz band, incredible musicians and flying birds, takes place in an extraordinary space that seems too large to fit inside an ordinary building. The ambassador's residence, Spaso House, was well known for containing a two-storey ballroom in its interior. For the duration of this scene, if not elsewhere, the cheeky talking cat Begemot appears as a projection of the impish Charles Thayer; the guests at Satan's ball, an unparalleled procession of murderers and pimps, represent the Soviet elite who came as the ambassador's guests; and Woland figures as an equivalent to Ambassador William Bullitt himself. To a large extent this is all just a bit of fun on Bulgakov's part, a private joke that very few people would ever notice. But in the context of his own situation in the 1930s, we can see how thrilling it must have felt when an all-powerful figure suddenly arrived in Moscow (travelling from the West, which might just as well have been another world in those days), singled out the writer, acclaimed him for his talent, and suggested he should come travelling outside of Russia. It was a rare thing by now for anybody to praise his talent, as Boris Pasternak had done at a party in that same spring of 1935, insisting that Bulgakov be toasted before Veresaev: 'Veresaev is of course a very great man, but he lives by the rules. Bulgakov goes beyond the rules!'[5] We can imagine just how much Bulgakov appreciated Ambassador Bullitt's comment about his work, when one day he called him 'a master'. This was an accolade he valued highly. Yelena had similarly paid tribute to the autobiographical features with which her husband had invested the hero of his greatest novel, by sewing him a round cap on to which she stitched the letter 'M' for 'Master'. Invitations continued to arrive for them after the ball in 1935, but in the aftermath of the March 1936 denunciation in *Pravda* and the taking off of the Molière play, Bulgakov and Yelena began to feel that it would be awkward to have to talk about their plight, and so they began to decline them. There were a few last social meetings with diplomats during April 1936, but the political situation felt increasingly precarious. Early in that same month Yelena also noted in her diary the arrest of their close friend Nikolay Lyamin, a scholar and librarian who had worked with Pavel Popov and was married to the artist Natal'ya Ushakova. Lyamin spent three years in exile, and was then rearrested in 1941, perishing in the camps.[6]

Apart from the social circle of foreign diplomats who seemed to value Bulgakov so highly, there was one other world where he felt appreciated and which had begun to open up for him before the catastrophic events of the spring of 1936, and that was the world of music. Bulgakov had retained his childhood passion for opera, and regular visits to the Bol'shoi to hear *Faust*, *Aida* and *Carmen* were still very important to him. After the emotionally draining experience of attending the first dress rehearsal of the Molière play on 6 February 1936, for example, Bulgakov went out to supper and then on to a performance of the opera *Sadko* at the Bol'shoi: 'M[ikhail A[fanas'evich] had a strong urge for music.'[7] Yelena described attending the dress rehearsal of Shostakovich's *Lady Macbeth of the Mtsensk District* (*Katerina Izmailova*) when it was first performed at Moscow's Nemirovich-Danchenko Theatre on 20 January 1934. She considered the music to be 'talented, original and unexpected'.[8] The theatre designer Vladimir Dmitriev, who had worked on the Art Theatre's production of Gogol's *Dead Souls* with Bulgakov and became a close friend, had been responsible for designing the Shostakovich opera as well. It was

Dmitriev who in October 1935 had brought Sergei Prokofiev to Bulgakov's apartment, on one of the composer's increasingly frequent visits to Soviet Russia from France, before he took the decision to return from emigration with his family in 1936. That was the occasion when there was a discussion of the possibility that Prokofiev might create an opera on the basis of Bulgakov's Pushkin play, and after listening to him reading, Prokofiev asked to take the text away with him and invited the couple to his concert the following day, where he played his recently completed ballet music for *Romeo and Juliet*.[9] The Bulgakovs were also becoming increasingly friendly at this time with Yakov Leont'ev, the deputy director of the Bol'shoi Theatre, and with one of the theatre's conductors, Aleksandr Melik-Pashaev (Bulgakov was particularly impressed by his magnificent tails too). After they had attended a further performance of Shostakovich's *Lady Macbeth* early in January 1936, brilliantly conducted by Melik-Pashaev, the Bol'shoi had approached Bulgakov with the suggestion that Shostakovich might be the composer to write an opera based on his Pushkin play. On 6 January they therefore entertained Leont'ev, Melik-Pashaev and Shostakovich at supper: Shostakovich was enthusiastic about the text, and after supper he played them the polka and waltz from his ballet of 1935, *The Bright Stream*. One can imagine the hopeful excitement Bulgakov must have felt at this moment, just when the Molière play looked as though it would finally reach the stage, to think that two of the most distinguished composers of the age were visiting him at home and seriously considering a collaboration that would give an entirely new musical life to his Pushkin play. All these hopes came crashing down, of course, with the devastating *Pravda* editorials singling Shostakovich out for attack on 28 January and 6 February, precisely for *Lady Macbeth* and *Bright Stream*, followed by the attack on Bulgakov himself on 9 March.

During the rest of 1936 the friendly contacts with Leont'ev, Melik-Pashaev and Dmitriev continued, and Dmitriev's next

'To my dear friend Yakov Leont'evich Leont'ev, from a loving M. Bulgakov'
(1 November 1937).

suggestion was that Bulgakov work with the composer Boris Asaf'ev on a new opera on a Russian historical subject, *Minin and Pozharsky*. The Artistic Director of the Bol'shoi, Samuil Samosud, was very persuasive, and Bulgakov completed the libretto in the space of four weeks, by the end of July 1936 (it never reached the stage). They followed this up with a further invitation, to rework the libretto of an opera by Sergei Pototsky. When Bulgakov announced in mid-September that he was leaving his post at the Moscow Art Theatre, the Bol'shoi leaped at the opportunity: 'We'll take you on in any capacity. Would you like to be a tenor?' said Samosud.[10] That October Bulgakov signed a contract to work as a librettist and literary consultant for the Bol'shoi, a post he would retain until the end of his life; and he also agreed to create a piece for them of his own, on a Civil War subject. This would become the libretto *The Black Sea*, which in many respects revisited the subject-matter of *Flight*. It depicts a young Russian couple in the Crimea during the later part of the Civil War, who are so appalled by White atrocities that they end up siding with the Reds and rejoicing at the departure of the Whites. This work, which was submitted to the theatre on 19 March 1937, is one of the most cautious works in both political and artistic terms in the Bulgakov canon – and it was never in fact staged as an opera.

Bulgakov's relations with the Bol'shoi Theatre remained positive throughout his association with them, which came as a great relief after the bitterness of his betrayal, as he saw it, by those at the Moscow Art Theatre who had failed to stand up for him when necessary. The work at the Bol'shoi offered many advantages, not least of which was the opportunity to become involved in the creation of opera and ballet, art forms which retained all the magic of theatre without exposing the author quite so nakedly to the risk of political attacks due to the content of his text. This turning towards a 'safer' genre was something many authors sought during the Terror, with the theatre director Meyerkhol'd also beginning to stage opera, and other writers resorting to relatively uncontroversial projects such as translating poetry or writing for children. During the spring of 1936, when things had become so difficult, Bulgakov had even considered entering a competition for the creation of a new textbook about the history of the USSR.[11] Bulgakov and Yelena were in and out of the Bol'shoi very frequently from 1936 onwards, attending most of their productions or at least dropping in to catch an act or two of whatever was on. Yelena was gratified to be given regular seats in the middle of the front row, where she and her children would be warmly welcomed by Melik-Pashaev from his conductor's desk, sparking the curiosity of her neighbours. The work provided a steady income, of course, and their friendships there flourished. The people they saw most regularly in the late 1930s were those involved in running the Bol'shoi (Samosud and Leont'ev, who was often so generous in providing cars for them to travel in); the conductor Melik-Pashaev and his wife; and stage designers such as Dmitriev, Piotr Vil'iams (who had designed the adaptation of *The Pickwick Papers* for the Art Theatre) and Boris Erdman, brother of the comic playwright Nikolay Erdman, who also became a particularly close friend.

The drawbacks of working for the Bol'shoi emerged only gradually. After the bright hopes of a possible collaboration at the highest artistic level with the likes of Prokofiev or Shostakovich, the reality turned out to be considerably more humdrum. In opera as in theatre there was continuous pressure to show that the Soviet era was capable of engendering important new works of art, and Bulgakov found himself either being invited to create new works with politically acceptable content for rather less distinguished composers such as Asaf'ev, or else – which was real drudgery – having to rewrite and improve other people's libretti that had turned out to lack artistic or stage qualities. Another feature of work at the Bol'shoi was that while certain meetings were scheduled for regular working hours, it was often difficult to get together with the artistic staff unless they met very late at night, after the day's performances were over – and Bulgakov would find himself setting off for meetings which began at midnight or even later. He tended to be a nocturnal creature in any case, so this pattern wasn't too difficult to manage; but on the other hand, it ate away still further into the time he could set aside for his own writings, including ongoing work on *The Master and Margarita*.

Bulgakov's acrimonious departure from the Moscow Art Theatre prompted him in January 1937 to continue the autobiographical story he had begun under the title *To a Secret Friend* in 1929. During the final stages of exasperation which he endured while Stanislavsky was rehearsing the Molière play, and also after his departure, he would come home from work and dash off a few pages of his *Theatrical Novel* while Yelena busied herself with organizing supper. Later in the evening, his friends would come round to hear the latest instalment of his mercilessly accurate satirical depiction of the goings-on in the Moscow Art Theatre: the rivalry between the two founders of the institution, his doubts about the acting 'Method' for which Stanislavsky would become so renowned, the extortionate ways of the finance and legal officers, the malicious gossip swirling around the secretaries' offices, the temperamental outbursts of the actors, and the astonishing perspicacity of the man who presided over the ticket office and knew within a split second of meeting someone whether he should grant them the privilege of a ticket. This proved a wonderful way for Bulgakov to vent his irritation, while providing his friends with hilarious entertainment. As time went on, however, his sense of resentment against the theatre grew more intense. Yelena had been indignant when the theatre failed to congratulate him on the six-hundredth performance of *The Days of the Turbins* in September 1935, and we have already seen how they also failed to mark the play's tenth anniversary in October 1936.[12] Further indignities followed, including articles and events marking the fortieth anniversary of the Art Theatre in 1938, which did not even mention his name, nor that of the play, even though it was the show that had been most frequently performed by the theatre during the Soviet era, reaching its eight-hundredth performance during 1938.[13] Bulgakov's despair began to centre increasingly on this almost surreal situation, in which everything he had ever undertaken was blocked, blanked out and ignored. There always seemed to be 'someone' in authority choosing to restrict his professional work, his actions and his opportunities – not to mention his ongoing attempts to travel abroad to deal with the occasional staging of his works in European theatres by people who did not scruple to distort his texts and pocket the profits. And as ever, there were tantalizing hints that perhaps Stalin himself was in fact more sympathetically disposed towards Bulgakov than his colleagues and minions. On 19 November 1936, when there were brief and inconclusive rumours that the decision about the Molière play might be reviewed, Leont'ev relayed a story that Stalin had been heard to say: 'What's all this about one of Bulgakov's plays being taken off? It's a pity – he's a talented author.'[14] Whatever Stalin's intentions, the effect of these rumours was constantly to raise Bulgakov's hopes that if he could just get to speak to the Leader, then his situation might be eased. Three days later Yelena Sergeevna recorded: 'We are having massages every day, it helps our nerves. We talk about our terrible life, and we read the newspapers.'[15]

There was of course much in the newspapers to alarm them as the Terror approached its most terrifying year, 1937. In Yelena's diary for that year there are many brief references to the flood of arrests going on all around them, affecting public figures and acquaintances, friend and foe alike. These included the Bol'shoi's director, Vladimir Mutnykh, who was accused in April 1937 of plotting terrorist actions against the government and promptly shot, and the Moscow Art Theatre's Artistic Director Mikhail Arkad'ev, who was arrested in June 1937 and shot shortly afterwards as a Polish spy; and writers such as Valentin Kataev, Bruno Yasensky, Adrian Piotrovsky and Boris Pil'nyak, all of them arrested that year along with nearly a dozen others mentioned in Yelena's diaries. Several of these were executed. There was ongoing anxiety shared with Akhmatova about the poet Mandel'shtam, whose wife also came to talk to Bulgakov in April 1937. Although they are not specifically mentioned, the year 1937 also saw the arrest of the country's top military commanders such as Marshal Tukhachevsky (tortured with seven others until he 'confessed', and then executed in June 1937). Some of them would have been known to Yelena personally, through her marriage to General Yevgeny Shilovsky. The late Maksim Gor'ky's personal assistant Pyotr Kryuchkov was caught up in one of the great show trials in 1937–8, in which many of Stalin's rivals were eliminated, including Rykov, Nikolay Bukharin and Yagoda. The fall of Yagoda and other highly placed members of the NKVD (formerly OGPU) is even briefly reflected in a detail in *The Master and Margarita*, where two new and unfamiliar figures bring up the rear of the long parade of guests arriving at Woland's ball, and it is explained that one of them has been accused of ordering the other to spray the walls of his successor's office with poison – an accusation that had been made in *Pravda* against Yagoda. When Yelena Sergeevna read of his disgrace on 4 April 1937, she exclaimed in her diary: 'It's joyous to think that Nemesis does exist for such people!'[16] Bulgakov himself, however, refused to allow himself the satisfaction of rejoicing over the downfall of his enemies (the playwrights Vladimir Kirshon and the RAPP leader Leopol'd Averbakh, arrested and shot; the playwright Aleksandr Afinogenov and the critic Osaf Litovsky, merely disgraced). Yelena's comment about Litovsky on 6 September 1937 was: 'Well, that would really be too good.'[17] Bulgakov notably refused to take part in any public actions or sign any denunciations to condemn those who had hitherto persecuted him. He brushed aside the words of those who tried to persuade him that his fortunes would now improve, and refused to take steps to ingratiate himself: 'I will not go to see anyone. I will not ask for anything.'[18] By May 1937 his fear of walking alone in the streets had returned.[19] On 23 September 1937 Yelena described his 'tormenting quest for a way out: a letter upwards? Should he abandon the theatre? Should he revise the novel and submit it? It's impossible to do anything. It's an utterly hopeless situation. We went on a river boat during the day – it soothes the nerves.'[20]

Despite his apprehensive thought of abandoning writing for the stage altogether, he was in fact persuaded by the Vakhtangov Theatre during 1937 to write a stage adaptation of *Don Quixote*. He completed the first draft by candlelight during the summer of 1938, in the rare happiness, peace and quiet of a summer holiday spent with Yelena in the provincial town of Lebedian', where he joined her once he had finished the full revision of *The Master and Margarita* in Moscow. That autumn the play, elegiac rather than comic in tone, was warmly received by the theatre, and even licensed for performance by the Repertory Committee. And then somehow, yet again, as Bulgakov wearily described it to his friend Veresaev, the actual production was delayed and deferred for reasons that remained a mystery, and it too was never actually staged in his lifetime.[21]

It was at this moment of renewed frustration and overwhelming exhaustion that he received a wholly unexpected visit in the late summer of 1938 from his former friends at the Moscow Art Theatre, imploring him to write a new play for them. The theatre had suffered the death of one of its founders, Stanislavsky, in the summer of 1938, and in general there was a sense of crisis about the repertory and about the theatre's direction. Their literary consultant Pavel Markov insisted that Bulgakov was the one dramatist who could rescue them. During painful meetings with them that August and September, Bulgakov poured out his anger and indignation about the treatment he had suffered at their hands, and despite their conceding how much he had been wronged, initially he refused to help. But they persisted, and suggested a theme that was of vital importance to their plans for the following year: in December 1939 Stalin would celebrate his sixtieth birthday, and cultural institutions would be expected to lay on appropriate events within the extremely tricky framework of the cult of personality.

Bulgakov eventually gave in, and agreed to write a play for the Moscow Art Theatre under the title *Batum*, describing the revolutionary activities of the young Stalin between 1898 and 1904, including his organizing of strikes in the small port of that name on the Black Sea, which Bulgakov had visited in 1921. This controversial work has been held by some commentators to represent a capitulation – possibly a shameful capitulation – to the dictates of Socialist Realism, and an opportunistic attempt on Bulgakov's part to curry favour with the authorities. Just how we are to evaluate the moral weight of such actions on the spectrum of compromises made by individuals with their consciences during the Terror remains, of course, a problematic question. Bulgakov's recorded interest in the subject actually dates back, somewhat surprisingly, to an earlier moment, to that same emotionally draining day on 6 February 1936 when the first dress rehearsal of the Molière play took place, and he sought out the relief of music afterwards by going to listen to *Sadko*. For that was also the day when the *Pravda* attack on Shostakovich's ballet music was published. Alongside his mood of tentative pleasure at seeing his play finally staged, the shock of the threat to Shostakovich must have been very troubling. Yelena's comments in her diary for that day include the brief remark that 'M[ikhail] A[fanas'evich] made a definite decision to write a play about Stalin.'[22] Several different factors must surely have shaped this new resolve. For one thing, Bulgakov was genuinely obsessed with the figure of Stalin, not just because of his enormous national significance, but because of the personal intervention he had made in Bulgakov's fate with his 1930 telephone call. He must also have been hoping that such a play would break through the wall of silence surrounding all his creative endeavours: if he could write something which passed the scrutiny of the censors, what theatre would dare to leave a work about the Great Leader gathering dust on the shelf? Perhaps too it would draw Stalin's favourable attention back towards him, and maybe he could after all obtain permission to travel abroad as his friend Zamyatin had done five years earlier. Another factor to bear in mind is that Bulgakov quite simply did not want to take on the role of a martyr, and the likelihood of that role being forced upon him had surely increased in the tragic period between 1936 and 1939, when the Terror had reached its unfettered heights.

The years 1938 and 1939 would indeed prove as traumatic as 1937, and Yelena's diary continued to chart a stream of arrests that swept away several more leading figures in the world of theatre and cinema, as well as many, many acquaintances, including their family doctor in February 1938 ('(!) What does all this mean?').[23] Bulgakov's opponent Kerzhentsev was disgraced in January 1938 (his assistant committed suicide ten days later). Very occasionally certain figures benefited from somewhat less harsh treatment: a relatively mild sentence of internal exile had been passed against Bulgakov's very close friend the playwright Nikolay Erdman, but in fact he managed to visit them in Moscow quite often, especially during Bulgakov's final illness. In February 1938, in the last letter Bulgakov actually sent to Stalin, he wrote not about his own plight but pleaded for Erdman's sentence to be eased. Vladimir Dmitriev shared with them his shock when his wife Yelizaveta was arrested on 6 February 1938, and Bulgakov helped him draft a plea to Stalin on 12 March. In fact Yelizaveta was executed some months afterwards, although Dmitriev only found out about that considerably later. In May 1939 the writer Isaak Babel' was arrested and tortured into 'confessing' links with the Trotskyite opposition; he was shot in January 1940. A particularly horrifying story was that of the great theatre director Vsevolod Meyerkhol'd, then in his mid-sixties, whose situation had become more and more precarious by the end of 1937, and whose theatre was closed down (by Kerzhentsev) in January 1938. Bulgakov's erstwhile theatrical rival was arrested on 20 June 1939; he was tortured and would eventually be shot on 2 February 1940. A letter he wrote to the Soviet premier Vyacheslav Molotov from prison, describing his beatings and torture in detail, has survived. Three weeks after his arrest his actress wife Zinaida Raykh was sadistically tortured and killed in their apartment by brutal assailants who were never brought to justice. This was widely interpreted as 'a warning to wives'.

This, then, is the immediate context against which Bulgakov sat down to work on his play about Stalin in January 1939. He drew on a number of historical sources, including a book called *The Batum Demonstration of 1902* published by the Communist Party publishing house in 1937 with a preface by Lavrenty Beria, who became head of the NKVD the following year.[24] The writing of the play went fairly smoothly, and he read various scenes to his friends and colleagues as he went along, doubtless in order to test their reactions to the content, and check whether his project was likely to prove acceptable. Work on *Batum* was completed on 24 July 1939.

In all the heated discussions that have taken place about the role of this play in Bulgakov's biography, its actual content has sometimes been rather ignored. Bulgakov clearly made a shrewd decision in not attempting to sum up the achievements of his main protagonist, as he had done previously by focusing on the last days of Molière, Pushkin, the Master and even Maksudov, the hero of his *Theatrical Novel* – for that kind of focus inevitably involves passing judgement on a career. Instead, he considered the very beginnings of Stalin's life as a revolutionary: his being thrown out of the seminary in Tiflis at nineteen years old, and his activities associated with the notorious strikes at the Rothschild oil refinery in 1902. If he had taken the subject of Stalin's later career he would have risked getting into very sensitive questions of the relations between Lenin and Stalin during the events of 1917 and their relative importance within the Bolshevik Party leadership, which it would surely have been impossible to navigate in safety. Questions have indeed been raised even about the accuracy of what was available to Bulgakov in the way of historical accounts of Stalin's actions during the Batum strikes, in prison and then Siberia, the period covered in the play, with the suggestion that Stalin might not have been too keen on any in-depth investigations of those details either. But when we read about Stalin in *Batum* the focus is simply on a young and charismatic figure with natural qualities of leadership, who inspires young people and workers to protest against the appalling conditions in which they work, and to call for an end to autocracy. As 'heroic tales' go, the result is a straightforward play with fairly convincing characterization and a reasonably well-structured plot; and within the range of flattering Soviet works about political leaders it stands as a relatively honourable and inoffensive piece of writing. If anything, the most crudely 'ideological' scene in the play is the one that depicts Tsar Nicholas II, showing him up as a man foolishly distracted by quack medicine and superstition, with a vindictive and bloodthirsty streak when it comes to suppressing opposition from the workers, and an obsession with training his pet canary to sing the national anthem. By contrast, one or two features of the depiction of Stalin could be said to be very cautiously controversial, not least the opening scene set in a seminary, which means that the spoken text of the play opens unexpectedly with a prayer ('Our true God . . .'), followed by the singing of a church choir. Stalin the ex-seminarist is even shown exclaiming to God in one scene.[25] There is also a curious and unflattering insistence on the police descriptions of him as having 'a particularly unremarkable appearance'.[26] What does represent a new departure for Bulgakov in this play is his turning away from all those inventive devices he had used in his drama previously, to introduce subjective perspectives and to heighten the dream-like, phantasmagorical aspects of plot. Instead we have a moderately socialist piece of realist writing.

As news got out about the play's completion, other theatres from around the Soviet Union (Kiev, Voronezh, Kazan') began to get in contact to ask if they too could see the text. When it was given a first reading at the Moscow Art Theatre on 27 July 1939 it was afforded a standing ovation, before being sent 'up' to Stalin's office for final approval. Early in August, the theatre asked Bulgakov to lead a team including assistant directors and designers to go and visit Tiflis and Batum to gain a sense of local colour for the production. On 13 August Yelena exclaimed in her diary: 'Are we really setting off tomorrow!! I can't believe my good fortune.' But the trip was to end in a catastrophe, which then became a tragedy. Two hours after their departure the train paused at a station called Serpukhov, and as they sat with two of their colleagues over breakfast in their compartment a postwoman appeared with a telegram from the theatre: 'Trip now unnecessary return Moscow.' The couple travelled on a little further, while they briefly considered whether to go south and try to take a holiday despite everything, but then they decided to get off and found a car to drive them back to Moscow:

> Misha was protecting his eyes from the sun with one hand, and with the other he held on to me and kept saying: what are we rushing back towards? Maybe towards our deaths? After three hours of frantic driving . . . we were back at the apartment. Misha wouldn't allow us to switch on the lights, so we lit candles. He walked up and down the apartment wringing his hands and saying – it smells of a corpse. Perhaps it is the corpse of my play? . . . Misha is in a dreadful state.[27]

A couple of days later they were visited by people from the Art Theatre who assured them that they would still meet the terms of their contract with Bulgakov, which involved the promise of a new apartment as well as a fee (neither of which ever materialized):

> And then they started to inform us that the play had received a harshly negative review up there (in the Central Committee, probably). It was not acceptable to turn a figure such as I. V. Stalin into a Romantic hero, it was not acceptable to place him in fictional situations and place invented words in his lips. The play could neither be staged nor published. And secondly, that up there they had viewed

Bulgakov's submitting of this play as representing a wish to build bridges and to improve attitudes towards him.[28]

Yelena indignantly repudiated these latter suggestions, although it is hard to believe that this was not to some extent what had motivated Bulgakov in agreeing to take on this project. As the month wore on, the sympathetic messages and visits from their friends did little to relieve their distress. In the background there were ominous events on the international scene, including the shocking news on 24 August of the signing of the Molotov–Ribbentrop Pact of Non-Aggression between the Soviet Union and Germany, swiftly followed of course by the outbreak of war in the West: 'Events are seething all around us, but they reach us only remotely, so struck down are we by our misfortunes.'[29] Yelena filled her waking hours with cleaning the flat thoroughly, while Bulgakov forced himself to do some foreign language exercises in a notebook; at earlier times of acute stress there had been a lot of card-playing and chess. 'Misha is in a depressed state. He says he has been utterly knocked off course. It has never been like this.'[30] There was some slight consolation in October, when the highly placed Soviet writer Aleksandr Fadeev came to let them know that during a visit to the Art Theatre Stalin had told Nemirovich-Danchenko that in fact he considered *Batum* to be a very good play, but that it would just not be appropriate to stage it. At least this meant that Bulgakov had not incurred Stalin's wrath with the work, even though it left him as ever in the uncertain position of having written something endorsed at the highest level, which still was not allowed to reach a theatre audience. By this point, however, he and Yelena were far more preoccupied with the rapidly worsening state of Bulgakov's health.

In September 1939 the couple travelled to Leningrad in the hope of getting some respite, as a substitute for their ruined trip to the south. But while he was there Bulgakov's sight, which had begun to cause anxiety at the beginning of the year and had got considerably worse since the traumatic events of that August, began to fail. As he told his sister Nadya, of whom he had seen rather little in recent years:

> I went out in the morning on to Nevsky Prospect and suddenly realized I could not see the signs. I went straight to a doctor. He advised me to return to Moscow immediately and have my urine tested. I said to my wife: 'You know, he has just pronounced my death sentence.'[31]

As a qualified doctor himself, he could not fail to recognize that his symptoms affecting his eyes and his kidneys were precisely the same ones that had characterized his father's malignant nephrosclerosis and caused his early death in 1907, at just about the same age as Bulgakov was now, in his late forties. Over the months that followed the disease took its unstoppable course, reducing him by November to moments of delirium and enormous physical discomfort, and later agony. It has been suggested that Stalin's awareness of Bulgakov's present plight, and intermittently benign attitude towards him, prompted the visit to the apartment from the literary mandarin Aleksandr Fadeev; and that Fadeev may have been the one who arranged for Bulgakov to spend a few weeks towards the end of 1939 in the Kremlin's new Barvikha sanatorium, reserved for the elite of Soviet society. But as the year came to an end he dictated a letter to a childhood friend from Kiev:

> So, now I have returned from the sanatorium. What is the matter with me? If I am to tell you candidly and in confidence, the thought is eating away at me that I have come back in order to die. This does not suit me for one reason: it is painful, tiresome and vulgar. As you know, there is only one decent way of dying, and that is shooting with a gun, but I do not possess such a thing, unfortunately.[32]

Bulgakov and Yelena with her son Sergei, and friends Popov and Marika Chimishkian, 27 February 1940.

At a later moment he would plead with Yelena to find out if her former husband would lend them a revolver.[33] All this was recorded in a diary Yelena kept of his illness, in which she noted his increasingly sporadic last words and phrases. There were moments of lucidity, when he was able to talk to family and other visitors (his sisters Nadya and Lyolya, Dmitriev, Vil'iams, the Erdmans and Boris Pasternak, whose presence he found comforting), and there were some touching photographs taken of him towards the end, surrounded by his wife Yelena and stepson Sergei, and intimate friends such as Pavel Popov. It was Popov who on 5 December 1939 wrote him the most loving tribute:

> I think of you constantly . . . Whether I see you or not, you are what adorns my life. I fear you may not suspect how much you mean to me . . . Reading the lines that you have written, you can be sure that a true culture of language still exists; when you journey in fantasy to the places which you have described, then you realize that the creative imagination has not dried up, that the flame which was lit by the Romantics, by Hoffmann

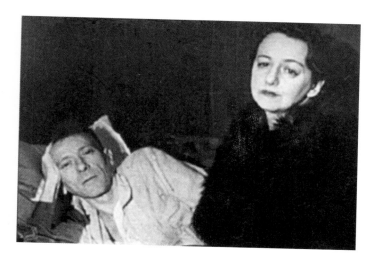

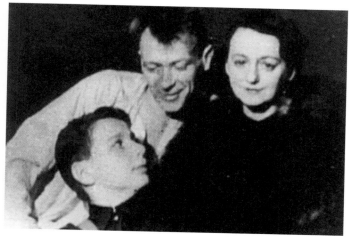

Bulgakov and Yelena, 27 February 1940.
Bulgakov and Yelena, with her son Sergei, 27 February 1940.

and others, burns brightly, and that in general the art of words has not been lost to people.[34]

That irrepressible impulse towards creativity was one of the last things to be extinguished in Bulgakov. During the grim autumn of 1939 he began to develop ideas for yet another new play, which he had first begun to think about in May. On 6 January 1940 he tried to write the beginning, but got no further than the opening stage direction: 'I can't write anything, my head is seething like a cauldron! I am ill, I am ill.' Although the play was notionally set in the Alhambra and called *Richard the Lionheart*, the outline of it as remembered by Yelena and Popov involved the encounter between a young writer and an NKVD officer, Richard Richardovich, who persuades him to prostitute his talent and write a play on a topic that will suit the authorities; but then Richard is himself arrested and the plans for the play are abandoned, leaving the writer ruined, imploring his disgusted wife to take him back.[35] All the dilemmas and anxieties of the previous year were still clearly troubling Bulgakov deeply.

One of Bulgakov's last ventures outdoors was on 13 January 1940, wearing his dark glasses and 'Master's' cap in the exceptionally bitter cold. By 24 January he was too exhausted to walk in the street by the time he got outside. As things became desperate, Yelena persuaded a group of the actors who had built their careers on *The Days of the Turbins* to write an appeal to Stalin, in which they described his plight and asked whether the Leader might not, as ten years earlier, speak to Bulgakov directly, in the hope that such a great event might restore his strength. There was no response.[36] On 28 January Yelena read to him from *The Master and Margarita* and he dictated corrections for the last time.[37] Thereafter he slipped towards the end with moments of irritability and great physical and mental distress, alternating with tender final words for Yelena, his Margarita. Bulgakov died on the afternoon of 10 March 1940.

Bulgakov wearing his dark glasses, 1939.

Epilogue

A question that has preoccupied some modern commentators is whether Bulgakov escaped the Terror for a reason that should cause us to condemn him as a self-serving compromiser. On the one hand, he sincerely placed his hopes in Stalin for many years, and in the Leader's capacity to intervene and ease his situation as he had done after the telephone conversation in 1930; and of course he did write the play *Batum* for the Moscow Art Theatre. On the other hand, he spoke out repeatedly to the Soviet authorities about his belief in freedom of speech, and continued to compose satirical works in private such as *The Master and Margarita* and his *Theatrical Novel*, in which he explored forbidden religious and social issues and emphasized the importance of subjectivity in art. He also refused, when asked, to sign any documents denouncing any of his acquaintances. It seems almost impossible to believe that, under the regime of close surveillance that prevailed in Moscow in the 1930s, the authorities were entirely unaware of the existence of *The Master and Margarita*. If they were aware of it, they never chose to act upon that knowledge; but clearly Bulgakov was liable to be hauled in at any point to answer for his creation. However distressing his final illness, perhaps it served at least to protect him from the danger of arrest and execution in the very late 1930s, and allowed him to die at home with his family. Like Anna Akhmatova, whose powerful account of the Terror in her cycle of poems called *Requiem* remained a closely guarded secret for decades, and like

Boris Pasternak, whose later novel *Dr Zhivago* stayed unpublished for so long, Bulgakov was allowed to live while so many others perished. And as with Akhmatova and Pasternak, his greatest works were published in Russia decades after their creation, surviving to fulfil his claim that 'Manuscripts don't burn.'

Yelena joined that extraordinary group of women, the Russian writers' widows including Osip Mandel'shtam's wife Nadezhda and Yevgeny Zamyatin's wife Liudmila who, having outlived their husbands, then dedicated themselves to preserving their works and their literary and personal archives until more liberal political circumstances made it possible for them to be published. Hitler's invasion of Soviet Russia in June 1941 naturally rendered the question of seeking further publications of Bulgakov's work unthinkable for the duration of the war. But on 7 July 1946 Yelena felt emboldened to address a letter herself to Stalin, claiming that Bulgakov himself had asked her to do this. She pointed out that *The Days of the Turbins* had finally been taken off after a thousand performances, and that the only works of her husband's still being staged at that time were his Pushkin play and his adaptation of Gogol's *Dead Souls*. She asked Stalin to intervene to allow for his works to be printed, in order to save his name from sinking into oblivion. But she received no response.[1]

However, the Thaw in cultural affairs that took place gradually after Stalin's death in 1953 saw the publication at last of some of his plays and stories, culminating in the abbreviated version of *The Master and Margarita* that appeared in the journal *Moscow* in 1966–7, followed by the full publication of the text in a volume containing all three of his novels in 1973. Both Tasya and Lyuba lived to see that edition of his novels published, whereas Yelena had died in 1970. She was buried alongside Bulgakov in the grave at the Novo-Devichy cemetery, where a boulder that had once adorned Gogol's grave had been placed at her request. The 1973 edition of the novel sold out in a flash, was pirated abroad, and changed hands on the black market

The grave of Bulgakov (1891–1940) and Yelena (1893–1970).

for many, many times its cover price. *The Master and Margarita* became a cult work, read at first in illicit, *samizdat* copies, and as time went by, in Soviet and post-Soviet editions with print runs of several million volumes at a time. It soon achieved such a level of popularity among Russian readers that it is fair to describe it as the most successful work of Russian fiction in the twentieth century.

Notwithstanding the rather unexpected gesture that the Soviet authorities had made in publishing *The Master and Margarita* during the Brezhnev era, they then made a protracted (although ultimately futile) attempt to limit further access to knowledge about Bulgakov's life and works. A few determined Russian scholars valiantly published as much as they could get away with over the following years, while the remaining unpublished works were printed in the West, and copies were sometimes smuggled back into the USSR. It would take until the *glasnost'* era under Gorbachev, for instance, for Soviet readers to be able to obtain legal copies of *The Heart of a Dog* (1987) and *Batum* (1988). Since that time, the archives have gradually been opened up to researchers, and full scholarly editions of Bulgakov's works have been produced.

It is difficult to imagine just how his career would have developed had Bulgakov lived in a society that had allowed his works to be published and staged before his death in 1940, rather than frustrating his every endeavour. It would be good to think that the ebullient inventiveness of his creative imagination would have flourished regardless of the pressures under which he was placed, and not in any sense because of them. His talent for the crafting of plot in his prose works was as original as were his ambitions for the stage in his drama, and his ease in switching back and forth between the two genres is neatly encapsulated in the ambiguous title given to his unfinished novel of the 1930s, *Teatral'nyi roman*: this can equally well be translated as *A Theatrical Novel* or *A Love-affair with Theatre*. In his own lifetime he was known almost exclusively as a dramatist; in the later twentieth century he became posthumously famous above all as a novelist. In this present century readers have continued to enjoy his stories, while as theatre spectators they have got to know his works not only through performances of his drama, but through a whole range of new stage adaptations of his prose, which continue to be inspired by its intensely dramatic qualities. We may recall again the words of Bulgakov's autobiographical hero from *A Theatrical Novel*, surely reflecting a deep-felt emotion: 'This world is my world . . .'.

Among the tributes received by Yelena after his death was a letter from Nemirovich-Danchenko assuring her that Bulgakov had not really died, for 'the strong and warm memory of him will last for many decades to come'.[2] Veresaev described him as 'the greatest contemporary dramatist'.[3] Dr Zakharov, who had attended Bulgakov in his final illness, told her that 'the honourable Russian intelligentsia of the transitional period [that is, pre- and post-1917] would never forget his achievements, since his thoughts and torments were those same reflections and suffering which they had shared'.[4] Pavel Popov, who sketched out a short biography of Bulgakov as early as 1940, wrote: 'Inquisitive and eternally searching, a man of restless intelligence and a rebellious spirit, he constantly worked upon himself: in his frequent hesitations and doubts he always managed to find a resolution, and never lost his nerve.'[5]

Perhaps one of the most striking comments came from within the literary establishment against which he had struggled for nearly twenty years. Aleksandr Fadeev, who occupied one of the top posts in the Writers' Union, apologized for not attending the funeral and insisted that this had no political significance. He was pleased to have met Bulgakov even at the end of his life, and passed a judgement on his achievements which must surely have echoed that of others within the establishment, including perhaps Stalin:

> It immediately became clear to me that before me was a man of astonishing talent, who in his inner being was honourable and principled, and very clever . . . People from the worlds of politics and of literature know that he was someone who never burdened himself in life or in his artistic work with any political lies, that his path was sincere and consistent; and if at the beginning of his career (and sometimes later) he saw things differently from the way they were in reality [that is, in Bolshevik interpretations], then there is nothing surprising about that. It would have been worse if he had been untrue to himself.[6]

References

1 Medicine and Literature, 1891–1921

1   For this opening chapter I have drawn extensively on the invaluable research of Bulgakov's niece, the linguistics scholar Yelena A. Zemskaya, *Mikhail Bulgakov i ego rodnye: Semeyny portret* (Moscow, 2004), as well as on studies such as Aleksei Varlamov's *Mikhail Bulgakov* (Moscow, 2008) and Boris Myagkov's *Rodosloviya Mikhaila Bulgakova* (Moscow, 2003).

2   Varlamov, *Mikhail Bulgakov*, p. 35.

3   Ibid., p. 36.

4   Ibid., p. 40.

5   See Zemskaya, *Semeyny portret*, pp. 96–7 and Myagkov, *Rodosloviya*, pp. 282–3. Varlamov suggests that she may have had a further abortion during 1917 (*Mikhail Bulgakov*, p. 70).

6   Zemskaya, *Semeyny portret*, p. 97.

7   Varlamov, *Mikhail Bulgakov*, pp. 62–5.

8   Myagkov, *Rodosloviya*, p. 286.

9   Ibid., pp. 286–9; Zemskaya, *Semeyny portret*, pp. 120–23; Varlamov, *Mikhail Bulgakov*, pp. 66–75.

10 Throughout this book I will be quoting Bulgakov's works in my own translation, using the eight-volume Azbuka edition (St Petersburg, 2011–13) as my source. Page references to the relevant volume are given after quotations in the text. The eight volumes are unnumbered, so I have given them Roman numerals, following roughly the chronological sequence of their contents. Full details of the contents of the eight volumes are provided in the Select Bibliography.

11 Letter of 30 October 1917 (VIII, 15).

12 Zemskaya, *Semeyny portret*, p. 77.

13 From the story *The City of Kiev* (1923), I, 296.

14 Quoted from J.A.E. Curtis, *Manuscripts Don't Burn. Mikhail Bulgakov: A Life in Letters and Diaries* (London, 1991), pp. 12–14.

15 Varlamov, *Mikhail Bulgakov*, p. 28.

16 Ibid., pp. 92–109, 112.

17 Ibid., pp. 115–16.

18 Ibid., pp. 121–4.

19 Zemskaya, *Semeyny portret*, p. 200.

20 From Bulgakov's 1924 *Autobiography*, quoted in Varlamov, *Mikhail Bulgakov*, p. 129. The story, which has not survived in full, was almost certainly based on the episode described in his mother's letter of late 1917, in which she described how she and Kolya came under fire.

21 Varlamov, *Mikhail Bulgakov*, pp. 131–2.

22 See E. J. Brown, *Mayakovsky: A Poet in the Revolution* (Princeton, NJ, 1973), pp. 54–6.

23 Zemskaya, *Semeyny portret*, pp. 272–3.

24 Ibid., p. 279.

25 Ibid., p. 274.

26 Ibid., pp. 275–7.

27 Ibid., p. 279.

28 Ibid.

2 Moscow, 1921–6

1 Yelena A. Zemskaya, *Mikhail Bulgakov i ego rodnye: Semeyny portret* (Moscow, 2004), pp. 169–70.

2 Letter to V. M. Voskresenskaya, 17 November 1921 (VIII, 40–41).

3 Aleksei Varlamov, *Mikhail Bulgakov* (Moscow, 2008), p. 185.

4 Letter to V. M. Voskresenskaya, 17 November 1921 (VIII, 39).

5 See the short story *A Recollection* for an account of this episode (I, 231–6).

6 Varlamov, *Mikhail Bulgakov*, p. 222.

7 *To a Secret Friend* (I, 389).

8   Varlamov, *Mikhail Bulgakov*, pp. 205, 206.

9   Letter to V. M. Voskresenskaya, 17 November 1921 (VIII, 38, 39).

10   Varlamov, *Mikhail Bulgakov*, p. 206.

11   *Forty Times Forty* (I, 275).

12   Ibid.

13   Diary, 2 September 1923 (VIII, 67–8).

14   Viktor Losev, ed., *Vospominaniya o Mikhaile Bulgakove* (Moscow, 2006), p. 318.

15   Boris Myagkov, *Rodosloviya Mikhaila Bulgakova* (Moscow, 2003), pp. 297–8.

16   Diary, 27 December 1928 (VIII, 101, 104).

17   Losev, *Vospominaniya*, p. 635.

18   The first parts of the novel were printed in *Russia*, 4 and 5 (1925).

19   Losev describes this episode in *Vospominaniya*, pp. 632–4.

20   Ibid., pp. 636–7.

21   Varlamov, *Mikhail Bulgakov*, pp. 333–6.

3 Four Plays, 1926–9

1   'October in the Theatre', in Yelena A. Zemskaya, *Mikhail Bulgakov i ego rodnye: Semeyny portret* (Moscow, 2004), pp. 180–82.

2   Aleksei Varlamov, *Mikhail Bulgakov* (Moscow, 2008), p. 361.

3   Anatoly Smeliansky, *Mikhail Bulgakov v Khudozhestvennom teatre*, 2nd revd edn (Moscow, 1989), pp. 67, 72–7, 84–6, 93.

4   Ibid., pp. 94–5.

5   Mikhail Bulgakov, *P'esy 20-kh godov*, ed. Aleksandr Ninov (Leningrad, 1989), pp. 144, 157, 159.

6   Smeliansky, *Bulgakov v Khudozhestvennom*, p. 106.

7   Varlamov, *Mikhail Bulgakov*, pp. 363–5.

8   Pavel Fokin, ed., *Bulgakov bez glyantsa* (St Petersburg, 2010), pp. 69, 237.

9   Smeliansky, *Bulgakov v Khudozhestvennom*, p. 86.

10   Fokin, *Bulgakov bez glyantsa*, p. 40.

11   Ibid.

12   Ibid., p. 39.

13   Ibid.

14 Ibid., p. 227.

15 Varlamov, *Mikhail Bulgakov*, pp. 365–6.

16 Ibid., p. 369.

17 Viktor Losev, ed., *Vospominaniya o Mikhaile Bulgakove* (Moscow, 2006), p. 352.

18 Varlamov, *Mikhail Bulgakov*, p. 367.

19 Ibid., pp. 379–81.

20 Bulgakov, *P'esy 20-kh godov*, p. 539.

21 See J.A.E. Curtis, 'Down with the Foxtrot! Concepts of Satire in the Soviet Theatre of the 1920s', in *Russian Theatre in the Age of Modernism*, ed. Robert Russell and Andrew Barratt (Basingstoke and London, 1990), pp. 219–35.

22 Rachmaninov set Pushkin's 1828 poem 'Do not sing, my beauty . . .' as one of his 'Six Romances' (Op. 4).

23 Bulgakov, *P'esy 20-kh godov*, p. 545.

24 Ibid., p. 546.

25 Varlamov, *Mikhail Bulgakov*, p. 382.

26 Ibid.

27 Ibid., p. 383.

28 Bulgakov, *P'esy 20-kh godov*, p. 569.

29 Ibid., p. 577.

30 Quoted in Bulgakov, *P'esy 20-kh godov*, p. 343.

31 Losev, *Vospominaniya*, pp. 368–71, 392–3.

32 Ibid., p. 403.

33 Varlamov, *Mikhail Bulgakov*, pp. 397–8.

34 Bulgakov, *P'esy 20-kh godov*, p. 556.

35 Losev, *Vospominaniya*, p. 667.

36 Ibid., p. 669.

37 Ibid., p. 670.

38 Ibid., pp. 672–3.

39 Varlamov, *Mikhail Bulgakov*, pp. 423–44.

40 Letters of 18 May, 24 June and 30 October 1926, and summer 1928 (VIII, 173–4, 180, 192–3, 229–30).

41 Letter to Nikolay Bulgakov, 24 August 1929 (VIII, 261–3).

4 'The Years of Catastrophe', 1929–36

1 *To a Secret Friend* (I, 375).
2 Pavel Fokin, ed., *Bulgakov bez glyantsa* (St Petersburg, 2010), pp. 278–9.
3 Ibid., pp. 281–2.
4 Ibid., p. 283.
5 Mikhail Bulgakov, *P'esy 30-kh godov*, ed. Aleksandr Ninov (St Petersburg, 1994), p. 565.
6 Article of 15 February 1936 for a Moscow Art Theatre publication, quoted in Bulgakov, *P'esy 30-kh godov*, p. 567.
7 Mikhail Bulgakov, *Pis'ma. Zhizneopisanie v dokumentakh*, ed. Viktor Losev and Viktor Petelin (Moscow, 1989), pp. 279–90.
8 Ibid., pp. 289–90.
9 Ibid., p. 294.
10 Aleksei Varlamov, *Mikhail Bulgakov* (Moscow, 2008), p. 489.
11 Ibid., p. 484.
12 Ibid., p. 492.
13 Ibid., pp. 497–9.
14 Ibid., pp. 501–2.
15 Ibid., pp. 505–7.
16 Ibid., pp. 508–9.
17 Ibid., p. 510.
18 Violetta Gudkova, ed., *'Kogda ya vskore budu umirat'...' Perepiska M. A. Bulgakova s P. S. Popovym (1928–1940)* (Moscow, 2003), pp. 19–34.
19 Varlamov, *Mikhail Bulgakov*, p. 511.
20 Gudkova, *Perepiska*, pp. 84, 88.
21 Ibid., pp. 117–19.
22 Ibid., pp. 99–102, 123–4.
23 Ibid., p. 116.
24 Ibid., p. 113.
25 Bulgakov, *Pis'ma*, pp. 361–2.
26 Varlamov, *Mikhail Bulgakov*, pp. 531, 533.
27 Ibid., p. 534.
28 Viktor Losev, ed., *Vospominaniya o Mikhaile Bulgakove* (Moscow, 2006), p. 421.
29 Bulgakov, *Pis'ma*, p. 353.

30   Varlamov, *Mikhail Bulgakov*, p. 541.

31   Bulgakov, *Pis'ma*, p. 364.

32   Varlamov, *Mikhail Bulgakov*, pp. 543–4.

33   Losev, *Vospominaniya*, p. 51.

34   Ibid., p. 109.

35   Ibid., p. 46.

36   Ibid., p. 42.

37   Letters drafted on 10–11 June 1934, Bulgakov, *Pis'ma*, pp. 429–39.

38   Nadezhda Mandel'shtam, *Vospominaniya*, ed. Yu. Freydin (Moscow, 1999), p. 187.

39   Bulgakov, *P'esy 30-kh godov*, p. 628.

40   Varlamov, *Mikhail Bulgakov*, pp. 643–54.

41   Gudkova, *Perepiska*, pp. 200–201.

42   Varlamov, *Mikhail Bulgakov*, p. 619.

43   Ibid., p. 630.

44   Ibid., pp. 639–40.

45   Letter of 2 October 1936, Bulgakov, *Pis'ma*, p. 367.

46   Gudkova, *Perepiska*, p. 215.

5 *The Master and Margarita*, 1936–40

1   For this account of the background to the creation of *The Master and Margarita* I have drawn on Viktor Losev's introduction to volume VII of Bulgakov's works, pp. 5–6.

2   Ibid., pp. 16–17.

3   Viktor Losev, ed., *Vospominaniya o Mikhaile Bulgakove* (Moscow, 2006), p. 82.

4   Diary entry for 23 April 1935, Losev, *Vospominaniya*, p. 85. For a fuller account of the significance of this event for Bulgakov, see J.A.E. Curtis, 'Mikhail Bulgakov and the Red Army's Polo Instructor; Political Satire in *The Master and Margarita*', in *'The Master and Margarita': A Critical Companion*, ed. Laura Weeks (Evanston, IL, 1996), pp. 211–26.

5   Losev, *Vospominaniya*, p. 82.

6   Ibid., p. 112; Boris Sokolov, *Entsiklopediya Bulgakovskaya* (Moscow, 1996), pp. 261–4.

7   Losev, *Vospominaniya*, p. 104.
8   Ibid., p. 39.
9   Ibid., pp. 96–7.
10 Ibid., p. 116.
11 Ibid., p. 109.
12 Ibid., p. 93.
13 Ibid., pp. 142, 211.
14 Ibid., p. 120.
15 Ibid.
16 Ibid., p. 134.
17 Ibid., p. 164.
18 Ibid., p. 146.
19 Ibid.
20 Ibid., p. 166.
21 Aleksei Varlamov, *Mikhail Bulgakov* (Moscow, 2008), pp. 755–9.
22 Losev, *Vospominaniya*, p. 104.
23 Ibid., p. 186.
24 Mikhail Bulgakov, *P'esy 30-kh godov*, ed. Aleksandr Ninov
    (St Petersburg, 1994), p. 645.
25 Ibid., pp. 212, 219.
26 Ibid., pp. 226, 227.
27 Losev, *Vospominaniya*, pp. 280–81.
28 Ibid., p. 281.
29 Ibid., p. 288.
30 Ibid., p. 285.
31 Varlamov, *Mikhail Bulgakov*, p. 779.
32 Ibid., pp. 782–3.
33 Ibid., p. 788.
34 Violetta Gudkova, ed., *'Kogda ya vskore budu umirat'...' Perepiska
    M. A. Bulgakova s P. S. Popovym (1928–1940)* (Moscow, 2003),
    pp. 234–5.
35 Varlamov, *Mikhail Bulgakov*, pp. 785–7.
36 Ibid., p. 789.
37 Losev, *Vospominaniya*, p. 293.

Epilogue

1 Mikhail Bulgakov, *Pis'ma. Zhizneopisanie v dokumentakh*, ed. Viktor Losev and Viktor Petelin (Moscow, 1989), pp. 545–57.

2 Ibid., p. 497.

3 Ibid., p. 499.

4 Ibid., p. 502.

5 Ibid., p. 543.

6 Ibid., pp. 500–501.

Select Bibliography

Russian Sources

Primary Sources
The most complete and authoritative Russian edition of Mikhail
Bulgakov's work is the eight-volume annotated edition edited by
Viktor Losev and published by Azbuka (St Petersburg, 2011–13).
The eight volumes are unnumbered, so for ease of reference I have
given them Roman numerals, following for the most part the
chronological sequence of their contents:

I   *Zapiski yunogo vracha. Morfiy. Zapiski na manzhetakh. Zapiski pokoynika.*
    (Avtobiograficheskaya proza) (The Notes of a Young Doctor; Morphine;
    Cuff Notes; Notes of a Dead Man (Autobiographical Prose))
    (St Petersburg, 2011)

II *Belaya gvardiya. Dni Turbinykh. Beg. (Roman, p'esy, stat'i, rasskazy)*
    (The White Guard; The Days of the Turbins; Flight (Novel, Plays,
    Articles, Stories)) (St Petersburg, 2011)

III *Sobach'e serdtse. D'yavoliada. Rokovye yaytsa* (The Heart of a Dog;
    Diaboliada; The Fateful Eggs) (St Petersburg, 2011)

IV *Ivan Vasil'evich. Zoykina kvartira. Adam i Eva. Aleksandr Pushkin.*
    (P'esy iinstsenirovki 20–30kh godov) (Ivan Vasil'evich; Zoyka's
    Apartment; Adam and Eve; Aleksandr Pushkin (Plays and Screen
    Plays of the 1920s–1930s)) (St Petersburg, 2011)

V   *Zhizn' gospodina de Mol'era. Kabala svyatosh. Poloumny Zhurden.*
    Skryaga. (Roman-biografiya, p'esy) (The Life of Monsieur de Molière;
    The Cabal of Hypocrites; Half-Mad Jourdain; The Miser (Biographical
    Novel, Plays)) (St Petersburg, 2011)

VI   *Master i Margarita* (The Master and Margarita) (St Petersburg, 2013)
VII *Knyaz' t'my. (Redaktsii i varianty romana 'Master i Margarita')* (The Prince of Darkness (Drafts and Variants of the Novel 'The Master and Margarita')) (St Petersburg, 2011)
VIII *Pod pyatoy: dnevnik. (Pis'ma i dokumenty)* (Under the Heel; Diary (Letters and Documents)) (St Petersburg, 2011)

Page references to the relevant volume are given after quotations in the text.

The fullest edition of Bulgakov's plays is the two-volume edition edited by Aleksandr Ninov:
Bulgakov, Mikhail, *P'esy 20-kh godov* and *P'esy 30-kh godov* (Leningrad, 1989; St Petersburg, 1994)

Bulgakov's correspondence is well represented in this volume:
Bulgakov, Mikhail, *Pis'ma. Zhizneopisanie v dokumentakh*, ed. Viktor Losev and Viktor Petelin (Moscow, 1989)

See also:
Gudkova, Violetta, ed., *'Kogda ya vskore budu umirat'...' Perepiska M. A. Bulgakova s P. S. Popovym (1928–1940)* (Moscow, 2003)

Secondary Sources
Fokin, Pavel, ed., *Bulgakov bez glyantsa* (St Petersburg, 2010)
Losev, Viktor, ed., *Vospominaniya o Mikhaile Bulgakove* (Moscow, 2006)
Myagkov, Boris, *Rodosloviya Mikhaila Bulgakova* (Moscow, 2003)
Sarnov, Benedikt, *Stalin i pisateli*, vol. II (Moscow, 2011)
Smeliansky, Anatoly, *Mikhail Bulgakov v Khudozhestvennom teatre*, 2nd revd edn (Moscow, 1989)
Varlamov, Aleksei, *Mikhail Bulgakov* (Moscow, 2008)
Zemskaya, Yelena, *Mikhail Bulgakov i ego rodnye: Semeyny portret* (Moscow, 2004)

All translations throughout this book are my own.

Recommended Reading in English

Barratt, Andrew, *Between Two Worlds: A Critical Introduction to 'The Master and Margarita'* (Oxford, 1987)

Curtis, J.A.E., *Manuscripts Don't Burn. Mikhail Bulgakov: A Life in Letters and Diaries* (London, 1991 and 2012)

—, *Bulgakov's Last Decade: The Writer as Hero* (Cambridge, 1987 and 2009)

Milne, Lesley, *Mikhail Bulgakov: A Critical Biography* (Cambridge, 1990)

—, ed., *Bulgakov the Novelist-Playwright* (Luxembourg, 1995)

Russell, Robert, and Andrew Barratt, eds, *Russian Theatre in the Age of Modernism* (Basingstoke and London, 1990)

Smeliansky, Anatoly, *Is Comrade Bulgakov Dead? Mikhail Bulgakov at the Moscow Art Theatre* (London, 1993)

Weeks, Laura, ed., *'The Master and Margarita': A Critical Companion* (Evanston, IL, 1996)

Note on Translations

Bulgakov's *Master and Margarita* has been translated with tremendous verve but a few inaccuracies by Michael Glenny. More accurate versions have been provided by Hugh Aplin, and by Diana Burgin with Katherine Tiernan O'Connor. The translation by Richard Pevear and Larissa Volokhonsky is not recommended.

In this book the transliteration of Russian names has been kept fairly simple, but academic convention has been respected to the extent that the soft sign in Russian has been represented in proper names by an apostrophe: so Gor'ky, Raskol'nikov, etc.

Acknowledgements

The centenary in 1991 of Mikhail Bulgakov's birth coincided with the year in which the Soviet Union was dismantled. A number of ground-breaking studies of Bulgakov's life and works had appeared in Russian and English before that date, and some were written for the centenary: many of those still provide excellent introductions to the author. It is a pleasure for me to acknowledge the help and inspiration I have been given by distinguished Bulgakov scholars over several decades, such as Marietta Chudakova, Anatoly Smeliansky, the late Aleksandr Ninov, Violetta Gudkova and Grigory Fayman in Russia, as well as Lesley Milne, the late Michael Glenny, Colin Wright, Edythe Haber and Ellendea Proffer in the West.

However, the gradual opening up of archives in the post-Soviet era has meant that new materials have emerged in the last 25 years, rounding out our knowledge of Bulgakov's wider family and their fates, but also revealing new and fascinating information about the workings of the Politburo and the OGPU/NKVD. Above all, it has become possible to gain a more nuanced understanding of Stalin's role in determining the fate of creative artists and their works. Editorial work by Viktor Losev has provided us with definitive textual resources, while studies of the author and his times by Aleksei Varlamov, Boris Myagkov, Benedikt Sarnov and others have contextualized that information. For the purposes of this biography I have chosen not to return to the pre-1991 studies, but to draw mainly on these post-Soviet works. For the most part, however, these sources are still available in Russian only.

The author would like to express enormous gratitude to Yury Krivonosov for his kind permission to re-use photographs from his book, *Mikhail Bulgakov. Fotoletopis' zhizni i tvorchestva* (Moscow, 2011).

I owe an enormous debt of love and gratitude to my family – Ray, Sasha and Jessica – who provided all kinds of support during the writing of this book, as well as shrewd editorial comments.

Photo Acknowledgements

The author and publishers wish to express their thanks to the following for illustrative material and/or permission to reproduce it. Some locations of works are given below rather than in the captions.

© Edition 'Richard' St Petersburg / Curtis Collection postcard: p. 10; © Everett Collection Historical / Alamy Stock Photo: p. 123; © Fine Art Images / Heritage Images / Topfoto: p. 142; © Heritage Image Partnership Ltd / Alamy Stock Photo: p. 84; © ITAR-TASS Photo Agency / Alamy Stock Photo: pp. 6, 17; from A. Konchakovsky and D. Malakov, *Kiev Mikhaila Bulgakova*, Mystetstvo (Kiev, 1990): pp. 15, 18, 37, 55; courtesy Yury Krivonosov, *Mikhail Bulgakov. Fotoletopis'zhizni i tvorchestva*, EKSMO (Moscow, 2011): pp. 14, 16, 20, 21, 50, 66, 87, 91, 93, 94, 95, 104, 105, 108, 129, 135, 144, 145, 146, 174, 175 (top and bottom), 177; © RIA Novosti / Topfoto: p. 70; © TASS / Topfoto: p. 143; from E. A. Zemskaya, *Mikhail Bulgakov i ego rodnye*, Yazyki Slavyanskoy Kul'tury (Moscow, 2004): pp. 12, 40.

under the following conditions:

you must attribute the work(s) in the manner specified by the author or licensor (but not in any way that suggests that they endorse you or your use of the work(s))

'share alike' – if you alter, transform, or build upon this work/these works, you may distribute the resulting work(s) only under the same or similar license to this one.